Marguerite Patten's
All-Colour Book of Freezing

D1421953

HAMLYN

LONDON · NEW YORK · SYDNEY · TORONTO

Published by
The Hamlyn Publishing Group Limited
London · New York · Sydney · Toronto
Astronaut House, Feltham, Middlesex, England
© Copyright The Hamlyn Publishing Group Limited 1975
ISBN 0 600 30266 0
Printed in England by Sir Joseph Causton and Sons Limited

Illustrated by Tony Streek
Jacket photograph by Paul Kemp
Polythene containers loaned by The Tupperware Company

Contents

continued overleaf

Useful facts and figures

Notes on metrication
In this book quantities have been given in both Imperial and metric measures. Exact conversion from Imperial to metric does not always give very convenient working quantities, so for greater convenience and ease of measuring we have taken an equivalent of 25 g. to 1 oz. for the dry measures and 6 dl. to 1 pint for the liquid measures. As a general guide, 1 kg. (1000 g.) equals 2·2 lb. or 2 lb. 3 oz.; 1 litre equals 1·76 pints or almost $1\frac{3}{4}$ pints.

Metric capacity of freezers
The metric capacity of freezers is measured in litres. To convert cubic feet to litres multiply by 28·30.

Oven temperatures
The following chart gives oven temperatures in degrees Fahrenheit and Celsius, and the Gas Mark.

Description	Fahrenheit	Celsius	Gas Mark
Very cool	225	110	$\frac{1}{4}$
	250	130	$\frac{1}{2}$
Cool	275	140	1
	300	150	2
Moderate	325	170	3
	350	180	4
Moderately hot	375	190	5
	400	200	6
Hot	425	220	7
	450	230	8
Very hot	475	240	9

Introduction

Probably no appliance has gained quicker popularity than a home freezer. When these first came on the market they were considered ideal for homes in the country where there would be an abundance of freshly grown vegetables and fruit. Undoubtedly many people still use their cabinets mainly for freezing these foods, but we have learned that a home freezer can store *practically* every food and will give you convenience and flexibility in catering that no other appliance will do.

What could be better than coming home tired and simply taking a complete meal from your freezer? Why not make larger quantities of dishes, eat the amount required on that particular day and freeze the remainder? Is it not a splendid thought that you can prepare food for Christmas or a party at your leisure and freeze it?

Freezing is undoubtedly the simplest form of food preservation. There are certain basic things to remember, i.e. freezing the food as quickly as possible, covering the food and efficiently following the instructions on defrosting etc., given by your manufacturer. If you do this you will be delighted with the results.

I have been fortunate enough to work with freezers for many years, indeed long before they were well established on the general market, and have lectured not only to users but to other home economists who have not had this previous experience. This means I have gathered together a great deal of information on freezing and the recipes given in this book are based on the kind of foods that I personally freeze at home. No two people use a freezer in exactly the same way so be prepared to experiment and remember *your* freezer is there to help you save time, money and effort.

Country pâté

□ *Cooking time:* 2¼ hours   □ *Preparation time:* 20 minutes
□ *Main cooking utensils:* ovenproof dish (about 1½-pint/1-litre capacity).
deep baking tin   □ *Oven temperature:* slow (300–325°F., 150–170°C.,
Gas Mark 2–3)   □ *Serves:* 6 as a main dish with salad, or up to 12
as an hors d'oeuvre
□ *Freezing tips:* it is better to freeze in small quantities so you will not
thaw out too much at one time. Wrap small containers in foil or
polythene. Seal firmly.   □ *Use within:* 6 weeks   □ *After freezing:*
allow to thaw out at room temperature (or see page 10).

3 bay leaves
4 rashers streaky bacon
1 lb./½ kg. pig's liver
8 oz./200 g. pork fat (belly of
pork good choice)
1 egg
1 oz./25 g. fine semolina

2 cloves garlic
pinch mixed herbs
½ level teaspoon ground mace
½ level teaspoon black pepper
1–2 teaspoons salt
2 tablespoons brandy

To cook

1 Well grease the dish and arrange the 3 bay leaves in the centre with the leaves pointing out to form a pattern (see picture).
2 Cover with the streaky bacon, neatly arranged, with the rinds removed.
3 Mince the liver and pork fat finely; add the beaten egg, semolina, finely chopped garlic, herbs, mace, pepper, salt and brandy.
4 Blend together well then turn into the prepared dish.
5 Stand the dish in a larger baking tin of water and cover with a lid, or aluminium foil. (This prevents the pâté drying.)
6 Bake in the centre of a slow oven until firm; keep in the container until quite cold. You can cover the top with a layer of melted butter.
7 To serve, cool, turn out and serve with hot toast and butter or with salad.

Variations: Use flour instead of semolina, or use calves' liver.
Add a little minced tongue to the liver, etc. For a creamy pâté add 3 tablespoons single or double cream.

To freeze

This pâté is better for freezing if made softer with cream as above. The basic recipe freezes very well, although the flavour of the garlic and brandy may be less obvious *after* freezing.

Freezing meat pâtés and offal: Most pâtés, whether home-made or bought, freeze well for a limited period. If they are kept several weeks longer than recommended they may dry slightly, in which case blend in a little whipped cream. Liver and most offal freeze excellently. Store for up to 3 months. Wrap securely in foil, polythene, etc., to prevent drying. Separate slices of liver with greaseproof or waxed paper so you can remove as much as you need. You can cook the liver from the frozen state.

Smoked haddock pâté

□ *Cooking time:* 10 minutes   □ *Preparation time:* 15 minutes
□ *Main cooking utensils:* saucepan, sieve or mincer   □ *Serves:* 6–8
□ *Freezing tips:* it is better to freeze in small quantities so you will not thaw out too much at one time. Wrap small containers in foil or polythene. Seal firmly.   □ *Use within:* 6 weeks   □ *After freezing:* allow to thaw out at room temperature, this takes several hours. To hasten defrosting, stand the container in *cold* water.

12 oz./300-350 g. smoked haddock
2 oz./50 g. butter
7½ oz. (12 tablespoons)/
  1½ dl. double cream
pepper, cayenne pepper
2 teaspoons lemon juice

1 teaspoon Worcestershire sauce
To cover
2 oz./50 g. melted butter
Garnish
parsley, lemon

To cook

1 Wipe the haddock and poach in boiling water for 10 minutes.
2 Drain the fish; skin and flake, then mash slightly.
3 Pass through a fine sieve or mincer, then blend with the melted or creamed butter. (You can put all the ingredients into the liquidiser (blender of the mixer) to make a pâté, but you will need to emulsify small quantities only at one time.) If not using the liquidiser continue as below.
4 Whip the cream until *almost* thick, fold in the fish and season well, tasting as you go. Add the lemon juice and sauce.
5 Pour into a dish, or individual serving dishes, and allow to set.
6 Serve with hot toast and butter. Garnish with parsley and lemon.

Variations: Use other smoked fish (cod's roe, smoked salmon, etc.) in place of smoked haddock – do not over-cook.

To freeze

I tend to make the pâté slightly softer than this recipe with 1–2 tablespoons extra cream; this compensates for the slight drying in freezing. Cover the pâté with a thin layer of melted butter, let this set, then cover. If pâtés are kept longer than recommended on the left, all that happens is that they tend to lose flavour and become dry.

Freezing fish pâtés and smoked fish: This fish pâté is very good for freezing and so are all fish pâtés. Freeze also, well-wrapped smoked salmon, trout, etc. Smoked haddock, kippers, etc. may be cooked from the frozen state.

Prawn cocktail
with soured cream sauce

□ *Preparation time:* 10 minutes   □ *Main utensils:* sharp knife, basin
□ *Serves:* 4
□ *Freezing tips:* put the prawns in one container or wrap in foil or
polythene. Put the sauce into another container (a covered yoghourt or
ice cream carton is excellent).   □ *Use within:* 1 month   □ *After
freezing:* allow to thaw out at room temperature, or stand the containers
in cold water to hasten defrosting.

½ lettuce
6 oz./150 g. shelled prawns
1 tablespoon fresh tomato purée*
few drops Worcestershire sauce
seasoning
1 carton soured cream or ¼ pint/
   1½ dl. fresh cream and
   1 tablespoon lemon juice

paprika (optional)
Garnish
4 whole prawns
4 lemon wedges

*Skin a large, ripe tomato and rub through a sieve; or emulsify in a blender.

To prepare

1 Shred the lettuce finely. Divide the lettuce and shelled prawns between four glasses.
2 Blend together the tomato purée, Worcestershire sauce, seasoning and soured cream.
3 Pour the sauce over the prawns and lettuce just before serving. Sprinkle with paprika if wished. Garnish with whole prawns and lemon slices, slit halfway up between the skin and the flesh so that they sit on the edge of the glass.

To freeze

Freeze freshly caught and cooked prawns or after skinning. It is better to freeze the prawns and sauce separately.

Freezing salad dressing and shellfish: Mayonnaise *does not* freeze, that is why this dressing is an excellent alternative. Shellfish freezes well. Skin prawns or shrimps ready for use; dress crab and freeze, or leave whole in shell. Lobster may be left whole in shell, or dressed. Use crab and lobster within 2 months. To hasten defrosting, put into cold water.

Grapefruit and prawn cocktail

☐ *Preparation time:* 10 minutes   ☐ *Main utensil:* sharp knife
☐ *Serves:* 4
☐ *Freezing tips:* prepare grapefruit as stage 1. Pack into small
containers or plastic bags. Prepare prawns and freeze separately. Do not
freeze lettuce or dressing.   ☐ *Use within:* grapefruit — 1 year, although
texture better if used within 6 months; prawns — 1 month   ☐ *After
freezing:* thaw out at room temperature, or stand the containers in cold
water to hasten defrosting.

4 grapefruit

8 oz./200–240 g. prawns or shrimps

Low-calorie dressing

4 sugar substitute tablets

1–2 teaspoons mustard

good pinch salt

shake pepper

2 tablespoons corn oil

2–4 tablespoons lemon juice

To prepare

1 Peel the grapefruit, remove the segments and put into a basin, discarding the pips and skin.

2 Add the peeled prawns (or shrimps), leaving four for garnish (keep the heads on these).

3 To make the dressing, crush the tablets (or you could use liquid sugar substitute), add the seasonings, then blend in the oil and lemon juice to taste.

4 Mix with the fruit and fish, then put into glasses and garnish with the whole prawns or shrimps. Serve as the first course of a meal.

Variation: Use a little sugar instead of sugar substitute.

To freeze

It is an excellent idea to buy grapefruit when inexpensive. Prepare them as stage 1 and freeze. Sugar or a sugar syrup may be added if desired. Pack in small containers so you have just enough for each meal.

Freezing citrus fruit: Citrus fruit may be frozen as grapefruit above, or squeeze the juice from the fruit and put into containers (allow about $\frac{1}{2}$ inch (1 cm.) headroom in containers for liquid juice to expand), or pour the juice into freezing trays; freeze as ice cubes, remove from the trays then pack in polythene bags.

Freeze finely grated rind (with or without sugar). Freeze sliced lemons for drinks, or whole oranges and lemons to make marmalade when convenient. If you are in a hurry, freeze whole citrus fruit; it is extremely easy to grate the rind when the fruit *is* frozen.

French onion soup

□ *Cooking time:* 1 hour   □ *Preparation time:* 15 minutes   □ *Main cooking utensil:* saucepan   □ *Serves:* 4–5
□ *Freezing tips:* pour soup into containers (allow $\frac{1}{2}$ inch (1 cm.) headroom at top of container to allow for expansion).   □ *Use within:* soup – 3 months; bread – 1 month   □ *After freezing:* thaw out at room temperature; this takes about 2 hours, or choose containers that may be put into very hot water to defrost the soup or that can be put on the cooker. Simply reheat, then add the bread etc., as stage 4.

1½ lb./¾ kg. onions
2 oz./50 g. butter or 1 oz./25 g.
    butter and 1 tablespoon oil
1½ pints/scant 1 litre beef stock
    or water and 2—3 beef stock
    cubes

seasoning
Onion soup gratinée
ingredients as opposite
4—5 rounds French bread
1½—2 oz./40—50 g. Gruyère or
    Cheddar cheese, grated

To cook

1 Peel and slice the onions thinly.
2 Heat the butter or butter and oil. Fry the onions until just golden but not too dark — it can take nearly 30 minutes, so care must be taken they do not burn. Keep pan covered and stir from time to time.
3 Add the stock and simmer for the rest of the cooking time; season.
4 **Onion soup gratinée:** When ready to serve, put pieces of bread or toast, or sliced French bread into individual soup cups; add the soup and grated cheese. Brown for a few minutes only under a hot grill — do not over-cook. Never use too much cheese otherwise you will have a tough stringy topping.

To freeze

Choose a rigid container or freeze in ovenproof basin, or stand polythene bags inside cartons (sugar packs excellent for this). Pour the soup into the container or basin or the supported bag, cool and seal. It is convenient to freeze rounds of bread too, ready cut to put on the soup (see page 111).

Freezing clear soups and stock: Never waste clear soups or stock, freeze as the method described above, or freeze concentrated stock (made by boiling down the liquid hard until strongly flavoured) in ice trays, then pack savoury cubes in polythene bags. Put 1 or 2 into a soup, stew or casserole to flavour. If recipe states 'add wine', try to add this when reheating *after* freezing, as some flavour of the wine is lost in freezing. Naturally, if freezing left-over wine-flavoured soup you cannot avoid this.

Cucumber soup

□ *Cooking time:* 30 minutes   □ *Preparation time:* 15 minutes
□ *Main cooking utensils:* large saucepan, sieve   □ *Serves:* 4
□ *Freezing tips:* pack as suggested on pages 16–17.   □ *Use within:* 2–3 months   □ *After freezing:* either thaw out the soup at room temperature (this takes 2–3 hours), or in the refrigerator (5–6 hours) and heat gently, or thaw sufficiently to tip out of the container or to heat very slowly in the freezing container.

18

1 pint/6 dl. white stock or water and chicken stock cube	seasoning
1 small cucumber	$\frac{1}{4}$ pint/1$\frac{1}{2}$ dl. milk
1 small onion	green colouring (optional)
1 oz./25 g. fat	*Garnish*
1$\frac{1}{2}$ oz./40 g. flour or $\frac{3}{4}$ oz./20 g. cornflour or 1$\frac{1}{2}$ oz./40 g. potato flour	parsley
	slices cucumber
	croûtons*

*To make croûtons, cut sliced bread into small dice, fry in hot butter or fat until brown; drain on absorbent paper.

To cook
1 Bring the stock to the boil. Cut 3–4 slices cucumber for garnish, peel the remainder and cut into $\frac{1}{2}$-inch (1-cm.) slices.
2 Chop the onion; add the cucumber and onion to the stock.
3 Cook gently until the cucumber is soft. Rub through a hair sieve, or emulsify in the liquidiser goblet.
4 Melt the fat in the saucepan, blend in the flour or cornflour or potato flour. Cook for 2–3 minutes.
5 Add the sieved cucumber gradually. Stirring all the time, bring to the boil and cook for 5 minutes. Season and add the milk; reheat, but do not boil.
6 Colour with a few drops of green colouring if the soup looks pale.
7 Sprinkle with chopped parsley and slices of cucumber just before serving. Serve croûtons separately.

To freeze
This soup can be made to the end of stage 6, cooled and frozen. Pack as suggested on page 17. There is a tendency for thickened soups to become thinner with freezing (less likely if you use cornflour or potato flour) so you may prefer to freeze the purée only and continue with the recipe from stages 4–7 when the purée has thawed out.

Freezing purée soups: This soup is typical of the method used for similar soups; if the soups contain cream add this after reheating if possible to avoid any likelihood of it curdling. Croûtons can be prepared and fried in large quantities then cooled, drained and packed (they do not stick together). Simply remove quantity required. Use within 3 months.

Trout rémoulade

□ *Cooking time:* 12 minutes   □ *Preparation time:* 15 minutes
□ *Main cooking utensil:* frying pan   □ *Serves:* 4
□ *Freezing tips:* either freeze uncooked fish, or cook to the end of
stage 4 then put the fish, nuts and any butter remaining in the pan
into dishes. Cool, cover and freeze. Do not freeze mayonnaise, but
freeze herbs.   □ *Use within:* uncooked fish – 4 months; cooked fish –
2 months; herbs – 6 months   □ *After freezing:* fry uncooked fish as
stages 1–4 – there is no need to defrost fish. If using cooked fish, then
just reheat for about 15 minutes in a moderately hot oven.

4 trout
seasoning
½ oz./15 g. flour
2–3 oz./50–75 g. butter
2–3 oz./50–75 g. blanched
    almonds
Sauce rémoulade
¼ pint/1½ dl. mayonnaise

½ teaspoon made mustard
2 teaspoons chopped herbs
    (parsley, chervil, tarragon,
    chives)
few capers
Garnish
watercress

To cook

1 Remove the heads from the fish and clean out the intestines.
2 Wipe well and dry, then coat lightly in seasoned flour.
3 Fry steadily for about 8 minutes in hot butter, then lift on to a hot dish.
4 Add the almonds to the butter remaining in the pan. Fry for a few minutes. Spoon over the top of the fish and garnish with watercress.
5 Serve hot with the cold sauce rémoulade – to make this, blend all the ingredients.

To freeze

Put the cooked fish into foil or flameproof dishes so that all you need to do is remove the food from the freezer and put it into the cooker.

Freezing freshwater fish and fresh herbs: Always ensure the fish is very fresh before freezing. Clean, remove heads if preferred; it is a good idea to wrap each fish as tightly as possible in foil or polythene (so you can use the number required), then to make a parcel of all the fish. You can also cook a larger quantity of fish than would be required for one meal and freeze the extra fish, ready to reheat. Herbs may be chopped, packed into small containers, covered, then frozen; or bunches of herbs may be frozen (wrapped or unwrapped). You can crumble the herbs if you do this *while they are still frozen*.

Scalloped prawns

☐ *Cooking time:* 30 minutes   ☐ *Preparation time:* 20 minutes
☐ *Main cooking utensils:* 2 saucepans, 4 scallop shells, large pipe and
piping bag   ☐ *Serves:* 4
☐ *Freezing tips:* if you use scallop shells, freeze the mixture first, *then*
cover with foil or polythene.   ☐ *Use within:* 1 month   ☐ *After
freezing:* reheat from the frozen state in a moderate oven.

Potato border
1 lb./½ kg. potatoes
seasoning
1 egg
1 oz./25 g. butter or margarine
2 tablespoons top of the milk
White sauce
1 oz./25 g. margarine
1 oz./25 g. flour
⅓ pint/2 dl. milk

seasoning
Filling
½ pint/3 dl. shelled prawns
½ teaspoon anchovy essence
1 dessertspoon lemon juice
½ teaspoon grated lemon rind
Garnish
few prawns, paprika pepper
parsley, lemon

To cook

1 Peel the potatoes and cook in boiling salted water until just tender.
2 Drain, mash well, sieving if necessary to give a very smooth mixture. Add the egg, butter and milk.
3 Put half the potato mixture into piping bag with a large pipe in position; pipe around the edges of the shells.
4 While the potatoes are cooking, prepare the sauce. Heat the margarine in a pan, stir in the flour and cook for several minutes.
5 Gradually add the milk, bring to the boil and cook until thickened, stirring.
6 Add the seasoning, chopped prawns, anchovy essence, lemon juice and rind, and the rest of the potato mixture.
7 Brown the potato edging under the grill.
8 Fill with the hot prawn mixture. Garnish with the remaining prawns, the paprika and parsley. Serve with wedges of lemon.

To freeze

Proceed as recipe above, but do not put the garnish on to the scallops before freezing. Pack the few prawns for garnish in a separate bag and place near the scallops so you can complete the dish.

Freezing potatoes: Raw potatoes cannot be frozen, but the method of preparation above is one excellent way of freezing potatoes (see also page 35).

Duchesse potatoes: Cook and mash potatoes as stages 1–2, but omit the milk. Add an extra egg yolk, if available. Pipe into rosette shapes on foil dishes or flameproof plates. Brush with a little egg white. Freeze, *then* cover. Heat and brown from the frozen state. Use within 6 months.

Mackerel in foil

☐ *Cooking time:* 30 minutes   ☐ *Preparation time:* 10–15 minutes
☐ *Main cooking utensils:* aluminium foil, baking sheet   ☐ *Oven temperature:* moderately hot (375–400°F., 190–200°C., Gas Mark 5–6)
☐ *Serves:* 4
☐ *Freezing tips:* simply check that the foil is firmly sealed around the fish. Cool, then freeze.   ☐ *Use within:* cooked – 2 months; uncooked – 3–4 months   ☐ *After freezing:* thaw out at room temperature for 2 hours, or several hours in the refrigerator if serving cold; otherwise heat for 15–20 minutes from the frozen state. If frozen without cooking follow timing above, allow a few minutes' extra cooking time.

4 small mackerel, about 8 oz./
   200 g. each
1 oz./25 g. butter
1 medium onion
1 tablespoon finely chopped
   parsley

1 tablespoon lemon juice
seasoning
Garnish
chives or parsley
lemon

To cook

1 Clean and wipe the fish. Remove the intestines but leave the heads on.

2 Cream most of the butter and add the chopped onion, parsley, lemon juice and seasoning.

3 Spread a quarter of the mixture into the cavity of each fish.

4 Cut four squares of aluminium foil, large enough to completely and loosely envelop each fish. Grease thoroughly with the remaining butter.

5 Lay the fish on the foil. Twist the edges and ends together securely to prevent the escape of juices.

6 Place on a baking sheet and bake just above the centre of the oven; do not over-cook if freezing.

7 Serve hot or cold with a green vegetable or salad. Garnish with chopped chives or parsley and lemon.

To freeze

It is an ideal plan to freeze fish, such as mackerel, which are only plentiful at certain times of the year. Either prepare the dish but do not cook, then freeze, or cook, as the recipe above, cool and freeze.

Freezing stuffings: The recipe above is a very simple stuffing but flavoured butters and stuffings of all kinds can be frozen. Mix, pack in useful-sized quantities in waxed containers, foil or polythene; label clearly. I find it useful to store all stuffings together in the freezer, so I can select exactly what I need quickly and easily.

Salmon steaks with soured cream sauce

☐ *Cooking time:* 15 minutes ☐ *Preparation time:* few minutes
☐ *Main cooking utensils:* foil, steamer, saucepan ☐ *Serves:* 4
☐ *Freezing tips:* separate steaks, see details on the right; wrap very firmly in foil or polythene. Used cream cartons or waxed containers are useful for this type of dressing. ☐ *Use within:* salmon – 4 months; cream dressing – 2 months ☐ *After freezing:* allow salmon steaks to thaw out at room temperature for 2–3 hours, or allow 4–5 hours in the refrigerator.

seasoning
4 salmon steaks
½ large cucumber
2 teaspoons lemon juice
2 cartons (10 fl. oz./3 dl.)
    soured cream or ½ pint/3 dl.
    fresh cream* and 2 tablespoons
    lemon juice

Garnish
tomatoes
lemon, watercress

*Use thin cream in this recipe rather than thick cream unless you intend to freeze the dressing (see below), when thick cream is better.

To cook

1 Season the salmon steaks and wrap in lightly greased kitchen foil; steam over boiling water for about 15 minutes. Do not over-cook.
2 Remove from the steamer and allow to cool; keep covered so they do not dry.
3 Slice the cucumber thinly. Arrange the cucumber slices on a dish and put the fish on top; garnish as the picture.
4 Blend the 2 teaspoons lemon juice with the soured cream, or the fresh cream and extra lemon juice.
5 Serve the salmon on a bed of salad. Either top with the sauce or serve it separately.

To freeze

Cooked salmon is liable to lose some of its texture so it is better to freeze raw salmon (see below). Obviously if you have cooked salmon left over it can be frozen. If you have any soured cream dressing left over, freeze this.

Freezing salmon and all types of cream: Salmon is a fish that freezes well. Cut it into convenient-sized pieces so you can take just sufficient for your needs from the freezer. Separate each slice (steak) of salmon with a square of greaseproof or waxed paper, then wrap very well. While you can cook salmon from the frozen state I find it better (because of the rather solid texture of the fish) to allow the salmon to defrost before cooking.

Cream can prove problematical in freezing. Do not try to freeze single (thin) cream. It must contain over 45% butter fat. Whipped cream is always satisfactory, provided it is well wrapped.

Swiss herrings

☐ *Cooking time:* 7–10 minutes ☐ *Preparation time:* few minutes
☐ *Main cooking utensil:* grill pan ☐ *Serves:* 4
☐ *Freezing tips:* use either frozen herrings and thaw out to bone and
add filling, or prepare and freeze, then cook from frozen state, or cook
(see right) and freeze. ☐ *Use within:* cooked fish – 2 months;
uncooked fish – 4 months ☐ *After freezing:* unwrap (but leave on the
foil) and cook, or reheat under a low grill or in the oven, then top with
the cheese and continue as the recipe.

4 herrings
seasoning
little oil
about 3 teaspoons French mustard
4 portions processed Swiss
  Gruyère cheese, or pieces
  Cheddar or Gruyère cheese

Garnish
parsley
lemon

To cook

1 Split open the herrings and remove the backbones. Season.
2 Oil the grill pan or foil (see under To freeze).
3 Brush the flesh side of the fish with French mustard and place under the grill for 3 minutes. Fold the herrings again.
4 When nearly cooked, arrange a portion of cheese horizontally on each fillet and continue gentle grilling until the cheese has melted and the fillets are cooked; do not over-cook.
5 Serve hot, garnished with parsley and lemon.

To freeze

First line the grill pan with four pieces of foil (one under each fish), then cook the fish to the end of stage 3 (do not over-cook). Cool, then lift the fish off the grill pan on to a flat tray. Freeze, then lift off the tray. Do not discard the foil but lay it and the fish on to fresh foil or polythene, or put into container and seal.

Freezing fried and grilled fish and cheese: Fish is not the most pleasant food to fry or grill, so I often cook more than I need (taking particular care not to over-cook it), then freeze and wrap immediately it is frozen. In this way you do not spoil the coating. Reheat when required.

Cheese freezes surprisingly well, although it may lose a little flavour; hard cheeses and blue cheeses tend to become a little drier and crumble slightly. Even so it is better to freeze the cheese than waste it. Wrap very firmly (see page 125) in foil or polythene. Use soft cheeses within 3 months; hard cheeses within 6 months.

Cod kebabs Ankara

□ *Cooking time:* 6–8 minutes   □ *Preparation time:* 15–20 minutes
□ *Main cooking utensils:* skewers, grill pan, saucepan   □ *Serves:* 4
□ *Freezing tips:* prepare the kebabs (with the exception of the tomatoes)
and freeze.   □ *Use within:* 6 months   □ *After freezing:* there is no
need to defrost, simply take the kebabs from the freezer, put the
tomatoes at the end of each skewer, and continue as from stage 6.

1½ lb./¾ kg. thick cod fillet	4 bay leaves
1 small green pepper	2 oz./50 g. butter, melted
4 small onions	salt
2 tomatoes	paprika pepper
4 button mushrooms	parsley

To cook

1 Cut the cod into large cubes.
2 Blanch the green pepper and onions by pouring on boiling water and leaving for 5 minutes (if freezing, blanch mushrooms for 1 minute only).
3 Drain and cut the pepper into cubes.
4 Quarter the tomatoes (omit at this stage if freezing).
5 Thread the fish cubes, vegetables and bay leaves on to four long metal skewers.
6 Brush all the ingredients with melted butter.
7 Season with salt and paprika pepper and grill for 6–8 minutes, turning once and brushing with more butter.
8 Serve sprinkled with parsley.

To freeze

Prepare the kebabs to the end of stage 5, but omit the tomatoes, which do not freeze. Wrap firmly. As the skewers may pierce the wrappings, the ends should be covered with thick foil or cardboard, or you could dice the fish, prepare vegetables, then pack and freeze.

Freezing white fish and tomatoes: White fish, like every kind of fish, must be very fresh if you intend freezing it. Cut into convenient-sized pieces: I should vary these – some fish can be diced for kebabs (as above), other fish cut into slices, more fish left whole, or in larger pieces for baking. Cover well – see page 27 for the way to separate slices of fish.

Tomatoes do not retain their shape if frozen, they collapse when thawed out. Even so it is worth freezing tomatoes as an uncooked or cooked purée. Pack as fruit juice or soup (see pages 15 and 17). If you freeze whole tomatoes you can skin them while frozen then use them for cooking. This is a very quick method if you have a glut; simply put the raw tomatoes into bags or containers, seal and freeze. Use purée within about 10 months, whole tomatoes within a year.

Aubergine gratinée

☐ *Cooking time:* 1¼ hours   ☐ *Preparation time:* 15 minutes, plus time
for aubergines to stand (to avoid a bitter taste from the skin)
☐ *Main cooking utensils:* frying pan, covered casserole   ☐ *Oven
temperature:* moderate (325–350°F., 170–180°C., Gas Mark 3–4)
☐ *Serves:* 4
☐ *Freezing tips:* cook the casserole up to the end of stage 6 – omit the
cheese at this stage. If more convenient, cook to the end of stage 8.
Cool, cover and freeze (see hints on right about lining casserole with
foil).   ☐ *Use within:* 6–8 months; with cheese topping: up to 6
months   ☐ *After freezing:* reheat gently from the frozen state if using a
suitable casserole, or foil (see right).

3 medium or 2 large aubergines
seasoning
1 oz./25 g. flour
4 oz./100 g. margarine or butter
4 large onions

4 large tomatoes
4 oz./100 g. cheese, grated
Garnish
chopped parsley

To cook

1 Wipe the aubergines; do *not* peel, then cut into thin slices. Sprinkle with a little salt and leave for 15 minutes.

2 Blend the seasoning with the flour and coat the aubergine slices.

3 Heat just over half the margarine or butter and toss the aubergine slices in this; do not allow to brown.

4 Lift out of the pan, add the rest of the margarine or butter.

5 Fry the thinly sliced peeled onions in this for 5—10 minutes, do not brown. Slice the tomatoes thinly and season well.

6 Put layers of aubergine, onion and tomatoes into the casserole with a sprinkling of the cheese on top; retain half the cheese for the topping.

7 Put a lid on the casserole and cook for 1 hour in the centre of the oven.

8 Remove the lid, sprinkle with remainder of the cheese and heat for a few minutes only. Top with parsley.

9 Serve as an hors d'oeuvre, or an accompaniment to fish or meat.

To freeze

Aubergine is a vegetable that only freezes *after* cooking and this is an ideal recipe in which to use aubergines.

Freezing casseroles: Casserole dishes may be put into the freezer. *If flameproof* (i.e. type of dish that may be used on top of the cooker or in the oven) you can take the dish straight from the freezer and put it into the oven or on top of the cooker — *over a gentle heat*. Do not have the heat too high otherwise the food burns before thawing.

If using an ovenproof casserole, you must allow dish and food to return to room temperature (this takes several hours). Casseroles are probably too precious to have in the freezer, so line the casserole with a double thickness of foil, then add the food as in recipe. Cook, freeze in casserole, lift out foil shape containing food, cover and store. Put back into the casserole to reheat.

Fried steak

☐ *Cooking time:* see stages 1 and 3 in recipe   ☐ *Preparation time:* few
minutes   ☐ *Main cooking utensil:* frying pan   ☐ *Serves:* 4
☐ *Freezing tips:* one cannot cook, then freeze, a steak, as it must be
freshly cooked then served as soon as possible after cooking. You can
fry or grill a steak from the freezer, *without* defrosting it; treat cutlets in
the same way.   ☐ *Use within:* steak – 6 months; vegetables – 6
months (see right-hand page)   ☐ *After freezing:* cook as timing on the
right, then serve with the prepared vegetables.

2 oz./50 g. fat, butter or oil   seasoning (optional)
4 portions entrecôte, fillet,
    rump or other prime steak

To cook

1 Heat the fat, butter or oil in the pan. Do not allow it to become too hot.

2 Put in the steak, it can be seasoned lightly if wished, and fry for times given below; turn with tongs or fish slice. Do not put prongs of fork into meat, as this allows the meat juices to run out.

3 Minute steak: 1 minute cooking each side.

Underdone steak ('rare'): About $\frac{3}{4}$ inch ($1\frac{1}{2}$ cm.) thick, 3 minutes on each side.

Medium-done steak: Cook as underdone, then lower heat and cook for further 2—3 minutes.

Well-done steak: Cook as underdone then lower heat and cook for further 4—6 minutes.

4 Serve with fried tomatoes, fried potatoes, mushrooms, broccoli spears and top with pats of parsley (maître d'hôtel) butter (made by adding a little lemon juice and chopped parsley to butter).

To freeze

Many butchers give reduced prices for bulk supplies of steaks and other meat so you can save money by buying larger quantities of meat. Wrap joints, steaks, cutlets closely in thick polythene or foil. Separate steaks etc. with squares of greaseproof or waxed paper or foil so you can peel off the number required at one time.

Freezing fried potatoes, mushrooms, broccoli: Peel potatoes, cut into slices or chips. Cook in very hot oil or fat until soft but not brown. Alternatively, cook in boiling salted water for 1—2 minutes (depending on thickness) only. Drain on absorbent paper; put on flat trays, freeze. Lift off trays, pack into containers and seal. Fry from the frozen state; use within 6 months.

Mushrooms are delicious if fried in a little fat or butter then cooled, packed and frozen; use within 6 months. For broccoli see page 71.

Darwin steaks

□ *Cooking time:* 15 minutes   □ *Preparation time:* 15 minutes
□ *Main cooking utensils:* frying pan, piping bag and potato pipe
□ *Serves:* 6–8
□ *Freezing tips:* prepare and cook the dish; freeze then cover – this
prevents the covering sticking to the tomato sauce.   □ *Use within:*
3 months   □ *After freezing:* reheat gently.

1½ lb./¾ kg. minced uncooked steak	seasoning
1 tablespoon mixed herbs*	1 oz./25 g. flour
1 tablespoon chopped parsley	2 oz./50 g. dripping
1 dessertspoon Worcestershire sauce	2 lb./1 kg. potatoes
8 oz./200 g. onions	½ pint/3 dl. tomato sauce
4 oz./100 g. bread	sprigs parsley
¼ pint/1½ dl. water	¼ pint/1½ dl. single cream (optional)

*Chopped freshly or use 1 teaspoon dried herbs.

To cook

1 Put the minced steak into a bowl with the mixed herbs, chopped parsley, Worcestershire sauce and chopped onions.
2 Cut the bread into pieces and cover with cold water.
3 Leave to soak through, then squeeze out most of the water.
4 Add the bread and seasoning to the meat mixture.
5 Shape into cakes and dust with seasoned flour. Heat the dripping.
6 Fry the cakes until brown on each side, then lower the heat and continue cooking. Meanwhile cook and mash the potatoes.
7 Pile or pipe the cooked mashed potatoes around the sides and at the bottom of an ovenproof dish. Put the meat cakes on top, with the tomato sauce, parsley and cream, if wished.

To freeze

It would be advisable to omit the parsley and cream before freezing then add these when the dish is reheated. Choose a flameproof dish that can go from the freezer to the oven or line dish with foil (see page 49).

Freezing complete meals: Busy people will find it an ideal arrangement to cook complete meals, put them into, or on to, dishes or individual plates (foil plates ideal), then cover with foil and freeze. Reheat in the oven when required. Freeze:
Sliced meat or jointed poultry in a sauce or gravy, or any casserole or stew with green beans or peas or carrots and creamed potatoes — if you have roast potatoes remove the cover from the potatoes only when reheating so they crisp.

Fried fish and chips — remove cover before heating so the food will crisp.

Store in the freezer for the shortest time recommended, e.g. if the fish should be stored for 2 months and the vegetables for 6 months, the complete dish should be stored for 2 months.

Mawarra meat curry

□ *Cooking time:* 3 hours   □ *Preparation time:* 30 minutes   □ *Main cooking utensils:* saucepan, casserole   □ *Oven temperature:* very moderate (325–350°F., 170–180°C., Gas Mark 3–4)   □ *Serves:* 4–5
□ *Freezing tips:* pack the mixture as suggestions on the right. Make quite certain that it is cold before freezing. Directions for freezing rice given on the right. Freeze this in a separate container from the curry.
□ *Use within:* curry – 3 months; rice – 4–5 months   □ *After freezing:* thaw out sufficiently to tip the curry into a pan to heat (this takes 1–2 hours) or put the flameproof casserole or foil dish into a low oven to reheat curry.

1¼ lb./generous ½ kg. chuck steak	¾ pint/4½ dl. stock
1 large onion	seasoning
1 oz./25 g. fat	2 oz./50 g. desiccated coconut
1–2 level tablespoons curry powder	2 oz./50 g. sultanas
1 level tablespoon paprika pepper	1 level tablespoon redcurrant
2 oz./50 g. walnuts, chopped	jelly
2 oz./50 g. blanched almonds	1 tablespoon lemon juice
1 oz./25 g. flour or ½ oz./15 g.	*To serve*
cornflour	8 oz./200 g. rice, boiled

To cook

1 Cut the meat into neat dice and fry with the chopped onion in the hot fat for 3–4 minutes.

2 Add the curry powder, paprika and nuts; cook for 3 minutes.

3 Stir in the flour and cook gently for several minutes.

4 Gradually blend in the stock, bring to the boil and cook until thickened. Season; add the coconut, sultanas, redcurrant jelly and lemon juice. Either cover the pan and simmer gently or transfer to a casserole, cover and cook in the centre of the oven.

5 Lift from the casserole and serve in a border of boiled long-grain rice. Serve sliced bananas, tomatoes and onion rings and sliced cucumber in yoghourt in separate bowls.

To freeze

Do not over-cook the meat as it will take 30–40 minutes to reheat slowly. When cold pack into waxed or polythene containers, foil dishes, polythene bags (supported by waxed containers until mixture is frozen) or freeze in the casserole (see page 33).

Freezing curries, meat stews, etc. and rice: The comments above apply to other casseroles. Use these within 2 months. I often find the flavour improves with keeping in the freezer. If the sauce has become a little thin, just stir in a little flour or cornflour blended with water or stock before serving. If cooking an extra large quantity, freeze in family-sized amounts.

Rice should be lightly cooked, cooled then packed loosely in containers. *Freeze until nearly hard* then break up the rice (use a fork if in a carton and handle briskly if in a sealed bag). Use within 4–5 months. Tip into boiling water or hot butter to reheat, or spread on a tray, cover and reheat gently in the oven. Frankly, I rarely freeze rice (only if I have some left over) as I feel it is so easily cooked, and it can lose some of its texture. Risottos with mixed vegetables, meat, fish, etc. may be frozen in the same way.

Polpette (meat balls) with Parmesan rice

☐ *Cooking time:* 20 minutes ☐ *Preparation time:* 15 minutes
☐ *Main cooking utensils:* deep fat pan, frying basket, saucepan
☐ *Serves:* 8
☐ *Freezing tips:* pack in containers, bags or foil when frozen; this prevents the balls sticking together, or the coating adhering to the polythene, etc. ☐ *Use within:* meat balls – 3 months; rice – 4–5 months
☐ *After freezing:* cooked meat balls – put on a flat baking tray (do not thaw out). Heat for about 6 minutes in hot oven, lower the heat for another 5–6 minutes. Uncooked meat balls – fry from the frozen state, then drain and serve. See page 39 for heating rice.

1 lb./½ kg. raw minced beef
2 tablespoons chopped parsley
¼ teaspoon nutmeg
grated rind of 1 lemon
2 slices bread, about ¾ inch/
   1½ cm. thick
2 eggs
2 cloves garlic
seasoning
Coating
1 oz./25 g. flour
1 egg

1–2 oz./25–50 g. crisp
   breadcrumbs
deep fat for frying
Rice mixture
4 oz./100 g. medium- or long-grain
   rice
just under ½ pint/3 dl. water
½ teaspoon salt
1 oz./25 g. butter
1–2 oz./25–50 g. grated
   Parmesan cheese

To cook

1 Mix together the meat, parsley, nutmeg and lemon rind.

2 Remove the crusts from the bread and soak this in beaten eggs until soft; mash with a fork and mix thoroughly into the meat mixture.

3 Halve and press the garlic cloves and add the juice only to the mixture; season generously.

4 Roll into little balls, using 1 good tablespoon meat mixture for each one. Flour lightly and coat twice with beaten egg and crumbs.

5 Fry in deep fat until golden and cooked. Drain on absorbent paper.

6 To boil the rice, put into a saucepan with the water. Bring to boil and add the salt. Lower the heat, cover the pan and cook steadily for 15 minutes, until all the water is absorbed and rice is tender. Add the butter and grated cheese. Serve the meat balls on the rice mixture.

To freeze

Either prepare to the end of stage 4, freeze on flat trays then pack, or fry and drain as stage 5, tip on the trays, freeze then pack. Boil the rice, do not add the butter or cheese, then freeze (see page 39). Tip the rice into the hot butter, stir over *low* heat until thawed out then add the cheese.

Freezing meat balls, meat cakes, etc.: Prepare all meat balls as above. Flat meat cakes, such as hamburgers, should be prepared, but not cooked; pack with a square of waxed or greaseproof paper between them so they do not stick together.

Coated cutlets and tomato dip

☐ *Cooking time:* 20 minutes   ☐ *Preparation time:* 15 minutes
☐ *Main cooking utensils:* frying pan, saucepan   ☐ *Serves:* 4
☐ *Freezing tips:* prepare the cutlets. Freeze as outlined on the right
(separate each cutlet before freezing), then wrap carefully, making
certain bones do not pierce the foil or polythene – twist extra foil
around these. Pack the cold dip into a polythene or waxed container.
☐ *Use within:* 6 months   ☐ *After freezing:* frozen food with an egg
and crumb coating fries extremely well so cook straight from the
freezer. Heat the dip as indicated on the right.

4 large or 8 small lamb cutlets
1 egg
3 tablespoons crisp breadcrumbs
Dip
1 medium onion
1 small apple
2 large tomatoes
1 oz./25 g. butter or margarine

1 small can or tube tomato purée
1 level teaspoon cornflour
$\frac{1}{2}$ pint/3 dl. water
seasoning
pinch sugar
pinch garlic salt
fat for frying

To cook

1 Coat the cutlets with beaten egg and crumbs.
2 Grate or chop the peeled onion and apple very finely. Slice the tomatoes. Fry in the hot butter or margarine for several minutes then add the tomato purée and cornflour blended with the water.
3 Bring the mixture to the boil and cook steadily, stirring well, until the mixture thickens slightly. Add the rest of the ingredients, lower the heat and continue cooking until a thick dip is formed.
4 Fry the cutlets in hot fat until crisp and golden brown; drain on absorbent kitchen paper or tissue paper. To serve for a barbecue, arrange the hot chops in a napkin-lined dish and serve the dip separately.

To freeze

You can freeze the dip when made up to the end of stage 3; in which case you may like to freeze it in a foil container which can be put into a slow oven to reheat; or just cook the onion, apple and tomatoes in the butter, put into a small polythene bag or carton and freeze. When you need the sauce, tip the onion, apple and tomato into a pan, add purée, water, etc. and make the sauce. It is always a good idea to coat cutlets, fish, etc. when you have a little spare time. Freeze on flat trays, lift off and pack in suitable containers. Remember to separate each cutlet with a piece of waxed or greaseproof paper.

Freezing dips and sauces: Provided a dip does not contain mayonnaise, which separates out during freezing, it will freeze well. This saves last-minute preparations for a party. If to be served cold, allow 2–3 hours at room temperature for about 1 pint (6 dl.) dip to thaw out. Most thickened sauces freeze well, particularly when cornflour or potato flour is used. Whisk sauce hard as it is reheated. If the sauce seems a little thin, then add a little blended flour or cornflour to thicken.

Lamb provençal

☐ *Cooking time:* 2–2¼ hours   ☐ *Preparation time:* 20 minutes
☐ *Main cooking utensil:* 2½-pint (1¼-litre) casserole   ☐ *Oven temperature:* very moderate (325–350°F., 170–180°C., Gas Mark 3–4)
☐ *Serves:* 6
☐ *Freezing tips:* cover the casserole tightly; when cold put into the freezer. See page 49 for details on lining casserole with foil.   ☐ *Use within:* 2–3 months   ☐ *After freezing:* if completely cooked before freezing I would prefer to thaw out before reheating (this takes several hours). If cooked to the end of stage 5 there is no need to thaw out; reheat for 30 minutes, remove the lid and continue cooking for another 30 minutes then raise the heat to moderate to brown the potatoes.

2 lb./1 kg. middle or scrag end
   lamb
1½ lb./¾ kg. peeled potatoes
12 oz./300 g. peeled onions
1 oz./25 g. butter

1 medium can tomatoes
seasoning
¼ level teaspoon dried mixed herbs
   or 1—2 teaspoons chopped fresh
   herbs

To cook

1 Cut the meat into convenient-sized pieces. Trim off the surplus fat.

2 Slice the potatoes and onions thinly.

3 Butter a casserole. Arrange in it layers of tomatoes, meat, onions and potatoes, seasoning each layer and adding herbs.

4 Pour over the juice from the tomatoes and finish with a layer of potato slices.

5 Pour in water to come halfway up the dish and spread butter over the top. Cover tightly and cook in the centre of the oven for 1½ hours. Make sure the lid does not press down on to the butter.

6 Remove the lid to brown the potatoes. Cook for a further 30 minutes. Serve with boiled carrots, tossed in butter and chopped parsley.

To freeze

If cooking this specially for freezing, I would cook only to the end of stage 5 (this saves any likelihood of over-cooking when reheating.) Cool, then cover the casserole and freeze. If more convenient, line the casserole with foil before adding the food (see page 49). If you have cooked this dish then decided to freeze it, take care, when reheating, that you do not over-cook it.

Freezing solid-type casseroles (hot-pots): This dish is typical of a hot-pot where you simply pack meat and vegetables in a dish and cook slowly. It is an excellent kind of dish to freeze but you must allow at least 1 hour in a *slow* oven to heat through if reheating from the frozen state.

Boiled silverside
with savoury dumplings

- ☐ *Cooking time:* see stage 2   ☐ *Preparation time:* 10 minutes
- ☐ *Main cooking utensil:* large saucepan   ☐ *Serves:* 6–8
- ☐ *Freezing tips:* either freeze the meat in the casserole with the vegetables, etc., or remove the meat, wrap well and freeze separately.
- ☐ *Use within:* 4 weeks   ☐ *After freezing:* reheat *gently* to avoid over-cooking the outside, or thaw out, then reheat.

3–4 lb./1½–2 kg. salt beef or
  silverside*
water
4 large onions
4 large carrots
1 bay leaf

Dumplings
4 oz./100 g. flour (with plain
  flour use 1 teaspoon baking
  powder)
good pinch salt
2 oz./50 g. shredded suet
½–1 tablespoon chopped herbs
water to mix

* Salted meat shrinks, so allow a good 8 oz. (200 g.) per person.

To cook
1 Soak the beef overnight in cold water. Put into fresh cold water.
Bring to the boil, add the onions, carrots and bay leaf.
2 Simmer very gently in a covered pan, allowing 30 minutes to
the lb. (½ kg.) and 30 minutes over.
3 To make the dumplings, sieve the flour and salt. Add the suet
and herbs and mix with enough water to form a sticky dough.
4 With floured hands, roll into balls. Add the dumplings to the
stock 15–20 minutes before the end of the cooking time.
5 To serve, lift the meat from the stock and arrange the dumplings
around. If liked, serve with a few carrots and onions. Serve a little
unthickened stock in a sauceboat.

To freeze
If you feel you may need this dish in a hurry, I would be inclined
to slice the silverside before freezing and put the sliced meat into
the liquid, or separate each slice with waxed or greaseproof
paper then wrap it well. This means you could serve the meat in
sandwiches, salads, etc.

Freezing salted meats: Salted and cured meats (including ham
and bacon) are at their best if stored for a shorter time in the
freezer than fresh meat. Store uncooked cured meats for up to 3
months and cooked cured meats for up to 1 month. Vacuum-
packed bacon can be stored for 3 months. Always wrap meats
very tightly and very well, see pages 125 and 127.

Moussaka

□ *Cooking time:* good 2 hours   □ *Preparation time:* 35 minutes
□ *Main cooking utensils:* large frying pan, covered casserole   □ *Oven temperature:* very moderate (325–350°F., 170–180°C., Gas Mark 3–4)
□ *Serves:* 4–6
□ *Freezing tips:* the cooked food cannot be turned into another container to freeze, so cook and freeze in foil dishes, or in the casserole or a foil-lined casserole, see right.   □ *Use within:* 3 months   □ *After freezing:* as this is such a solid dish, thaw out slightly if possible before heating, otherwise heat very slowly. Ovenproof dishes cannot be put straight from freezer to oven.

3 oz./75 g. butter
8 oz./200 g. onions
2 large aubergines
1–1½ lb./½–¾ kg. potatoes
Sauce*
1–2 oz./25–50 g. butter
1–2 oz./25–50 g. flour
½–1 pint/3–6 dl. milk

seasoning
2–4 oz./50–100 g. cheese, grated
1–2 eggs
1 lb./½ kg. minced lamb, mutton or beef
2–4 tomatoes
parsley

* Use the larger quantities if you like a moist dish.

To cook

1 Heat the butter and fry the sliced onions until tender but not broken. Remove the onions, then fry the sliced aubergines and thinly sliced potatoes, turning until well coated.
2 To make the sauce, heat the butter and add the flour; cook for several minutes, then gradually add the milk.
3 Bring to the boil and cook until thickened and smooth; add the seasoning, grated cheese and beaten egg – do not cook again.
4 Arrange a layer of the sliced aubergine and potato in the dish, top with the well seasoned meat, onion and sliced tomato.
5 Put a small amount of sauce on each layer; continue filling the dish ending with potatoes, aubergine and sauce.
6 Cover the dish and cook for 1½ hours. Garnish with parsley.

To freeze

Cool, then freeze. I generally use a foil-lined dish if I cannot spare the casserole for freezing. To line a dish with foil put a double sheet of ordinary foil or single sheet of thicker freezer foil into the casserole. Mould to the shape of the dish. Leave a good rim on top so you can lift out the foil, etc. Fill with food, cook as above. When ready to freeze fold over rim on top and cover with a lid of foil. Seal, freeze and remove from casserole.

Carbonnade de boeuf
à la flamande

□ *Cooking time:* 2¼ hours   □ *Preparation time:* 15–20 minutes
□ *Main cooking utensil:* large saucepan or casserole   □ *Oven
temperature:* very moderate (325–350°F., 170–180°C., Gas Mark 3)
□ *Serves:* 4–6
Freezing tips: I prefer not to cut the meat into too small pieces so it
retains its texture.   □ *Use within:* 2 months   □ *After freezing:*
reheat thoroughly, see page 45.

4 large onions
$1\frac{1}{4}$–$1\frac{1}{2}$ lb./$\frac{5}{8}$–$\frac{3}{4}$ kg. stewing beef
2 oz./50 g. dripping or fat
1 oz./25 g. flour
seasoning
2 oz./50 g. lean bacon, chopped

$\frac{1}{2}$ pint/3 dl. beer
$\frac{1}{2}$ pint/3 dl. stock*
1 teaspoon mustard
2 teaspoons sugar
bouquet garni

* If cooking in a casserole, use only $\frac{1}{4}$ pint ($1\frac{1}{2}$ dl.) stock.

To cook
1 Cut the onions into thin slices and the meat into strips.
2 Fry the onions in the hot fat until golden brown.
3 Coat the meat in the seasoned flour, fry for several minutes. Add the rest of the ingredients. Bring to the boil, stirring well, and cook until a smooth sauce.
4 Either transfer to a covered casserole and cook for approximately 2 hours at temperature given, in the centre of the oven, or lower the heat, cover the pan tightly and cook for approximately the same time.
5 Serve with boiled potatoes, or this is extremely good with boiled noodles and a green vegetable or sauerkraut.

To freeze
Cook up to end of stage 4, then cool. Pack into a container or leave in the casserole (see page 33), cover and freeze.

Freezing uncooked meats: Many people save money by buying meat in bulk at an appreciably lower cost than the usual retail price. You may well have to take a selection of various joints if you buy in this manner, i.e. stewing meat, prime roasting joints, steaks or cutlets, etc. plus offal. If this method of buying does not appeal to you, always have some uncooked meat in your freezer to save last minute shopping. Have convenient sized pieces, wrap tightly and well (see pages 125 and 127). Use beef and lamb within 9 months, pork within 6 months, veal within 4 months. If the meat is rather fatty I would remove surplus fat before freezing, or use the meat in a shorter time than suggested above. Personally I am always slightly disappointed with frozen veal and try to use this quickly, or not to freeze it. I find large joints are more tender if thawed out *before* cooking but tend to shrink less if you cook from the frozen state at a lower temperature than usual. This means a longer cooking period — about 50% longer.

Roast game

☐ *Cooking time:* see stages 2 and 3 in recipe   ☐ *Preparation time:* few
minutes for the bird only   ☐ *Main cooking utensil:* roasting tin
☐ *Oven temperature:* hot (425–450°F., 220–230°C., Gas Mark 7–8)
☐ *Serves:* allow 1 small or ½ medium bird per person; for larger game,
divide as chicken or turkey.
☐ *Freezing tips:* wrap uncooked game well; put the giblets in small
polythene bags and wrap with the game, using thick or a double layer
of foil.   ☐ *Use within:* 6–8 months   ☐ *After freezing:* thaw out before
cooking; this takes up to 12 hours at room temperature, or 24 hours
(for large pheasants) in a refrigerator.

Some of the most usual game are: capercailzie (wild turkey), cygnet (young swan – rare), golden plover, grouse, hare (can be roasted with stuffing as duck), leveret (young hare), ortolan, partridge, pheasant, pigeon, quail, snipe, rabbit, teal (wild duck), venison (deer), widgeon, woodcock

To cook

1 Make certain the game is really young for roasting. Cover the breast of the game bird with plenty of fat bacon, butter or fat to keep it moist – see also stage 4. Baste, i.e. spoon the fat over this during roasting, unless using foil or a covered roasting tin.

2 If using either of these allow an extra 15 minutes' cooking time, or have an electric oven 25°F. (12°C.) higher or a gas oven 1 mark higher. Use the hottest part of the oven.

3 Allow 15 minutes per lb. ($\frac{1}{2}$ kg.) and 15 minutes over; reduce the heat slightly for larger birds after the first 30 minutes, or use slower cooking as pages 54 and 55.

4 A knob of butter, a little cream or blue cheese inside the bird keeps it very moist and gives extra flavour.

5 Venison should be marinated for at least 24 hours in red wine plus a little oil and seasoning, lifted out of this liquid, then roasted at the temperature on left for 40 minutes then the rest of the time in a moderate oven. Allow 25 minutes per lb. ($\frac{1}{2}$ kg.) and 25 minutes over.

6 Serve with thickened gravy, bread sauce, or redcurrant jelly; game chips – made by frying wafer-thin slices of potato, and fried crumbs – made by frying fairly coarse crumbs in butter.

Freezing game: Allow game to hang for the usual period before freezing and thaw out thoroughly (see left) before roasting. Fried crumbs may be frozen following the instructions for croûtons, see page 19.

Pheasants in Calvados

□ *Cooking time:* 1 hour 20 minutes   □ *Preparation time:* 15 minutes
□ *Main cooking utensils:* roasting tin and foil, or deep casserole,
saucepan   □ *Oven temperature:* moderately hot (400°F., 200°C., Gas
Mark 6), then moderate (350–375°F., 180–190°C., Gas Mark 4–5)
Serves: 4–6
□ *Freezing tips:* I am not a great believer in freezing cooked game as it
tends to be dry; but if you want to freeze this dish see directions on the
right.   □ *Use within:* 1 month if possible   □ *After freezing:* thaw out
the pheasants; reheat thoroughly and complete the cooking, basting
well. Heat the sauce, then add the cream and continue as the recipe.

2 pheasants
3 oz./75 g. cream cheese
about 20 grapes
2 oz./50 g. butter
¼ pint/1½ dl. Calvados
1 oz./25 g. flour or potato

flour or ½ oz./15 g. cornflour
½ pint/3 dl. stock*
¼ pint/1½ dl. thick cream
seasoning
Garnish
grapes, watercress

* Use good beef or pheasant stock.

To cook

1 Wash and dry the pheasants then stuff with the cream cheese and seeded and skinned grapes.
2 Heat the butter in the roasting tin or casserole, turn the pheasants in this. Cook for 20 minutes until golden coloured in the hottest part of a moderately hot oven.
3 Add the Calvados, cover the tin loosely with foil (do not wrap the birds) or put lid on the casserole. Lower the heat.
4 Continue cooking for 1 hour at a moderate heat.
5 Lift the pheasants from the cooking container on to a hot dish and keep hot. Strain the liquid into the saucepan; blend the flour or cornflour with the stock. Add to the liquid and cook gently, stirring well, until the sauce thickens slightly.
6 Remove from the heat, whisk in the cream and heat *without boiling*; season well.
7 Coat the pheasants with a little sauce and garnish with seeded grapes and watercress. Serve with cooked celery or celeriac and Brussels sprouts. Pour the remaining sauce into a sauceboat.

To freeze

Follow the recipe to the end of stage 4, but allow 40–45 minutes only. Lift pheasants from the tin or casserole, cool and wrap separately. Make the sauce as stage 5 but omit the cream (stage 6). Freeze in a separate container.

Freezing sauces: There are many people who say 'never freeze a sauce, it could separate out or it could curdle.' If it helps you to have the sauce made beforehand or if you have sauce left over that could be wasted, then freeze it. Sauces thickened with potato flour or cornflour rarely curdle. If the sauce becomes a little too thin after freezing, heat gently and add a little extra thickening just before serving, see page 43. If any sauce has curdled, i.e. separated out, whisk very briskly as you heat it, or emulsify in the liquidiser and return to the pan.

Fried chicken
with mustard filling

☐ *Cooking time:* 15 minutes   ☐ *Preparation time:* 15 minutes
☐ *Main cooking utensil:* large frying pan   ☐ *Serves:* 4
☐ *Freezing tips:* whichever method you choose for freezing this dish,
i.e. raw or cooked, freeze the coated chicken on a flat tray before
covering, so the crumb coating does not stick to the wrapping.   ☐ *Use
within:* raw prepared chicken – 5–6 months; cooked chicken – 2–3
months   ☐ *After freezing:* if serving cold, thaw out at room temperature
for 2 hours, or 4–5 hours in the refrigerator, otherwise cook or reheat
from the frozen state.

4 joints young frying chicken,
  preferably breast
Filling
2 oz./50 g. butter or margarine
2 oz./50 g. soft breadcrumbs
2 teaspoons chopped parsley
4 teaspoons French or made
  English mustard

Coating
1 egg
2–3 oz./50–75 g. crisp
  breadcrumbs
To fry
3 oz./75 g. fat
Garnish
lettuce, lemon

To cook

1 If using frozen chicken joints allow these to defrost, then cut away the bones from the breast.

2 Mix the filling ingredients together, slit the poultry joints to form a pocket and spread the mustard filling in this.

3 Coat the joints with beaten egg and crumbs.

4 Heat the fat, cook the coated chicken quickly on either side until crisp and brown.

5 Lower the heat and continue cooking until tender, or see comments under 'To freeze'.

6 Drain on absorbent paper. Serve hot or cold with lettuce and thick wedges of lemon.

To freeze

Either prepare to the end of stage 3 and freeze coated but raw chicken, or fry as stages 4 and 5. If you intend to reheat this in the oven, fry until crisp and brown, but not entirely cooked.

Grilled chicken

☐ *Cooking time:* 15–20 minutes   ☐ *Preparation time:* 5–8 minutes
☐ *Main cooking utensil:* grill pan   ☐ *Serves:* 4
☐ *Freezing tips:* wrap uncooked chicken or chicken joints very firmly; the tighter the wrap the quicker the freezing time and the better the texture of the bird.   ☐ *Use within:* 12 months   ☐ *After freezing:* grill while still frozen; there is no need to thaw out joints before cooking.

4 joints young chicken
1–2 oz./25–50 g. butter
seasoning
squeeze lemon juice (optional)
Additional accompaniments
whole or sliced mushrooms

whole or halved tomatoes
little butter
seasoning
bacon rashers
parsley

To cook

1 Put the joints of chicken on to the grid of the grill if you can get this a reasonable distance away from the grill. If the grill compartment is very shallow, it is better to put the chicken in the actual grill pan.

2 Brush with a little melted butter and season lightly; a squeeze of lemon juice adds flavour.

3 Heat the grill, put the chicken under. Allow 4–5 minutes on either side with the grill at maximum heat.

4 Turn the heat lower and allow a further 8–12 minutes.

5 Grill sliced or whole mushrooms and/or tomatoes at the same time. Brush the vegetables with melted butter and season. Add chopped or whole rashers of bacon during cooking and cook until slightly crisp.

6 Serve on a hot dish with the mushrooms etc. around or over top of the chicken joints. Garnish with parsley.

To freeze poultry

If you can purchase very good quality poultry, prepare the birds for cooking (draw, truss, etc.). Pack the giblets in a polythene bag, then wrap well in thick foil or polythene – see the drawing on page 57.

To defrost poultry

Allow plenty of time for whole birds; large chickens or small turkeys take at least 24 hours in refrigerator. Only small chicken joints should be cooked from the frozen state.

Chicken casserole bonne femme

☐ *Cooking time:* $2\frac{1}{4}$–$2\frac{1}{2}$ hours   ☐ *Preparation time:* 30 minutes
☐ *Main cooking utensil:* large saucepan   ☐ *Serves:* 6–8
☐ *Freezing tips:* it is easier to wrap this if the whole chicken is lifted out of the liquid, drained, cooled and wrapped, then the vegetable mixture frozen separately.   ☐ *Use within:* 2 months if potatoes and cream are not added; 1 month if the complete dish is prepared.   ☐ *After freezing:* allow the chicken etc. to thaw out, add to the vegetables, etc. and heat gently.

chicken liver	2 turnips, diced
8 oz./200 g. pork sausage meat	6 carrots
mixed herbs	seasoning
1 boiling fowl	2 bay leaves
1 oz./25 g. butter	sprig sage or pinch dried herbs
1 tablespoon oil	sprig thyme or pinch dried thyme
small amount diced celery	4–6 potatoes
few celery leaves	little cream (optional)

In the picture the herbs are shown loose, but they are easier to remove if tied in a bouquet garni.

To cook

1 Blend the diced raw chicken liver with the sausage meat and herbs and put into the chicken. Tie or skewer firmly.
2 Heat the chicken in the butter and oil until golden.
3 Add all the rest of the ingredients, except the potatoes and cream.
4 Cover the pan tightly and simmer gently for $1\frac{1}{2}$ hours.
5 Add the finely diced potatoes and continue cooking for a further 30–45 minutes.
6 Lift the chicken on to a dish with the whole vegetables.
7 Remove the herbs and beat the potatoes into the stock to make a sauce, adding a little cream and extra seasoning if required. Serve hot with the other vegetables.

To freeze

Cook the fowl, etc. lightly at stage 4. I like to freeze at that stage and add the potatoes and cream when reheating this dish.

Some suggestions for covering food for the freezer

Use double thickness foil or freezer (heavy) foil, or foil dishes (obtainable in various shapes and sizes).

Use heavy polythene or ordinary polythene and another covering of foil, or polythene boxes with lids.

Use waxed cartons, etc. (these can be used again); cream cartons, etc. are excellent for short-term storage but rather poor quality for longer storage.

Use ovenproof ware (be careful to allow to return to room temperature after being in freezer and before putting in the oven), or flameproof ware (the type that can go on the cooker as well as in the oven), which can go from the freezer to the cooker.

Devilled chicken

□ *Cooking time:* method 1 – 20–25 minutes; method 2 – 1 hour 15 minutes   □ *Preparation time:* method 1 – few minutes; method 2 – 20 minutes   □ *Main cooking utensils:* method 1 – grill pan; method 2 – large saucepan, smaller pan   □ *Serves:* 4–6 (both methods)
□ *Freezing tips:* method 1 – you can cook the chicken joints from frozen state. Method 2 – thaw the chicken before cooking.
□ *Use within:* method 1 – 3 months; method 2 – 2 months, or 1 month if cream is added to the sauce.   □ *After freezing:* method 1 – serve at once; method 2 – if the entire dish has been prepared then frozen, thaw out and then heat *very gently.*

4–6 joints frying chicken
2 oz./50 g. butter, melted
Devilled crumb mixture
4 oz./100 g. soft breadcrumbs
2 oz./50 g. soft butter
1 tablespoon made mustard

1 teaspoon curry powder
1 small chopped onion or
 shallot
pinch cayenne pepper
Garnish
lemon wedges

Method 1 *(Illustrated left)*
To cook
1 Cut the chicken into serving pieces.
2 Brush the pieces with the melted butter and grill for 10–15 minutes until nearly tender.
3 Blend two-thirds of the crumbs with the remaining ingredients for the devilled mixture and press firmly over the top of the chicken pieces. Press the remaining crumbs on top and continue grilling slowly for a further 10 minutes. Garnish with lemon.

Method 2
1 Put a defrosted chicken into a pan with water to cover, sliced vegetables, herbs and seasoning to flavour. Simmer for 1 hour until just tender.
2 Lift the bird out carefully and strain off $\frac{1}{2}$ pint (3 dl.) stock for the sauce.
3 Joint the bird and slice the breast if fairly solid; keep warm.
4 To make sauce, melt 1 oz. (25 g.) butter, stir in $\frac{1}{2}$ oz. (15 g.) cornflour, 1 teaspoon made mustard, 1 teaspoon curry powder and the $\frac{1}{2}$ pint (3 dl.) chicken stock.
5 Bring to boil and cook until thickened, stirring. Stir in 2 tablespoons double cream blended with 1 beaten egg.
6 *Simmer* for 2–3 minutes. Season and pour over the chicken.

To freeze
Dishes like this are amazingly versatile. Either freeze the cooked chicken before jointing, or joint and freeze, or coat the chicken with the sauce and freeze in a flameproof casserole or foil dish.

Chicken terrine

☐ *Cooking time:* 1 hour for stock, 1½ hours for terrine   ☐ *Preparation time:* 30 minutes   ☐ *Main cooking utensils:* saucepan, 2-lb. (1-kg.) loaf tin, tin for water   ☐ *Oven temperature:* slow to very moderate (300–325°F., 150–170°C., Gas Mark 2–3)   ☐ *Makes:* 8–10 portions as first course, or 5–6 as main course
☐ *Freezing tips:* either cool, then cover the tin tightly with thick foil or polythene wrap, or freeze in the tin (cover this), then turn out of the tin and wrap.   ☐ *Use within:* 8–10 weeks   ☐ *After freezing:* see pâté, page 8

3½–4 lb./1¾–2 kg. roasting
   chicken with the giblets*
seasoning
bouquet garni
8 oz./200 g. lean ham

3 oz./75 g. blanched almonds
2 tablespoons brandy
3 tablespoons thick cream
2 oz./50 g. butter

*Omit the giblets for a milder flavoured stock.

To cook

1 Cut the raw chicken flesh from the bones; keep the chicken skin. Simmer the bones and giblets with seasoning, bouquet garni and water to cover in the pan for 40 minutes.

2 Remove the lid, boil until only ¼ pint (1½ dl.) stock is left. Strain carefully.

3 Cut the breast into neat slices, mince all the rest of the meat with the ham. Blend with half the stock, the coarsely chopped nuts, brandy, cream and seasoning.

4 Spread a generous layer of butter over the sides and bottom of the tin. Arrange a third of the sliced chicken and stock on this then half the minced mixture.

5 Add another third of the sliced breast and stock and the rest of the minced mixture.

6 Top with the last of the sliced chicken, stock, chicken skin and butter. Cover with foil, stand in a tin of cold water and cook at temperature given.

7 Remove from the oven, put a weight on top and leave to cool; if any stock rises to top of the tin pour this away. Remove the chicken skin when cold. Serve sliced with toast and salad.

Variation: Use game instead of chicken.

Freezing poultry, game and meat moulds: A terrine or mould is an excellent recipe for parties so it is wise to make and freeze ahead (to save last-minute preparations). Wrap well and do not store for too long a period, see left.

Guinea fowl and prunes

☐ *Cooking time:* 2¼ hours   ☐ *Preparation time:* 15 minutes, plus overnight soaking of prunes   ☐ *Main cooking utensils:* saucepan, large covered casserole   ☐ *Oven temperature:* very moderate (325–350°F., 170–180°C., Gas Mark 3–4)   ☐ *Serves:* 4

☐ *Freezing tips:* either line a casserole with foil (see page 49) before stage 4, or cook in a flameproof casserole (*do not over-cook*), cool and wrap well.   ☐ *Use within:* cooked dish — 1 month (guinea fowl is dry-fleshed so should not be frozen for too long a period); if freezing raw guinea fowl, use within 3 months.   ☐ *After freezing:* thaw out for 4–5 hours at toom temperature or overnight in refrigerator; heat gently but very thoroughly to complete the cooking.

4–6 oz./100–150 g. prunes
1 large or 2 small guinea fowl
seasoning
1 oz./25 g. flour
1 oz./25 g. fat or dripping
1 large onion, sliced

4–6 oz./100–150 g. pickled
  pork or cured bacon
1 small cabbage
1 wine glass red wine
4 smoked sausages or rashers
  bacon

To cook

1 Soak the prunes overnight in cold water; drain and remove the stones.

2 Roll the bird in seasoned flour and fry in the hot fat or dripping until golden.

3 Remove the fowl. Fry the sliced onion and pork for 5 minutes.

4 Shred and wash the cabbage. Mix with the onion and diced pork or bacon, season well and put half at bottom of the casserole.

5 Put the bird and some prunes on this, cover with the cabbage mixture and prunes; add the red wine. Arrange the smoked sausages or extra bacon on top, cover with a lid and cook for 2 hours.

6 To serve, lift the bird from the casserole, carve or joint and arrange prunes etc. around. Serve with new or creamed potatoes and a green vegetable. No sauce is needed.

To freeze

Cook as the recipe, but allow only 1½ hours at stage 5.

Freezing dishes with wine: Wine and all alcohol may lose a little flavour in freezing, so where a recipe adds this during the last stages of cooking I always try to freeze the recipe without the wine etc. and add it when reheating. Where a recipe uses wine as an essential ingredient (as in the recipe above), then I am a little 'mean' with this and add more when reheating if I feel the dish *has* lost some flavour.

Goose and chestnuts

□ *Cooking time:* see method   □ *Preparation time:* 25 minutes
□ *Main cooking utensils:* saucepan, roasting tin □ *Oven temperature:* moderately hot (400°F., 200°C., Gas Mark 6) then lower heat, see method   □ *Serves:* 8–10
□ *Freezing tips:* see right-hand side. Goose — wrap giblets in separate polythene bag, put with goose. Wrap very tightly to follow shape of bird (see page 58).   □ *Use within:* stuffing and nuts – 1 month. Goose – 4–5 months (duck – up to 6 months)   □ *After freezing:* allow the stuffing to thaw out (this will take about 1–2 hours at room temperature). Mix with the diced liver, then continue as the recipe.

1½ lb./¾ kg. chestnuts or 1–2 cans chestnuts
4 rashers streaky bacon
3 large onions
3 oz./75 g. butter or margarine
2–3 cooking apples
2 teaspoons chopped fresh sage
seasoning
goose liver

1 goose (about 10 lb./5 kg. when trussed)
goose giblets
1½ pints/9 dl. water
3 tablespoons goose fat
2 oz./50 g. flour
¼ pint/1½ dl. red wine
2 teaspoons chopped herbs
Garnish
watercress

To cook

1 Slit the chestnuts and boil for 5–10 minutes in water.
2 Cool enough to handle then remove the skins. Or drain canned chestnuts.
3 Chop the bacon; peel and slice the onions. Heat the butter or margarine. Fry the onions until slightly softened then add the bacon and cook for a few minutes.
4 Blend with half the chestnuts, the peeled diced apples, sage, seasoning and the diced raw goose liver.
5 Put into the goose and place in the tin.
6 Cook for 15 minutes per lb. (½ kg.) (weight when stuffed) and 15 minutes over. (If preferred cook in a moderate oven only and allow 25 minutes per lb. (½ kg.) and 25 minutes over.)
7 Prick from time to time to allow the fat to run out, and lower the heat slightly after about 40 minutes.
8 Simmer the giblets in the water to give a stock; strain well.
9 To make the sauce, heat the goose fat, stir in the flour and cook for several minutes. Gradually blend in 1¼ pints (7½ dl.) stock, bring to the boil and cook until thickened. Add the rest of the chestnuts, the wine and chopped herbs.
10 Place the goose on a serving dish and garnish.

Variation: Use duck instead of goose.

To freeze

This is a recipe where it is a good idea *not* to freeze the complete dish but to freeze some of the ingredients for use later.
a I would proceed up to stage 4, but omit the liver. Pack this mixture into a carton and freeze it.
b I would freeze remaining chestnuts in a small container.
c I would freeze a goose if I could buy it cheaper before Christmas or other holiday period, or if supplies were not to be relied upon.

Peas with bacon

□ *Cooking time:* see stage 1   □ *Preparation time:* few minutes
□ *Main cooking utensils:* saucepan, frying pan   □ *Serves:* 4
□ *Freezing tips:* pack the cooked dish in polythene, or a waxed container
□ *Use within:* cooked dish – 4–6 weeks. Uncooked, but blanched peas
1 year   □ *After freezing:* heat a knob of fat in a pan, add the frozen
peas, etc. and toss in fat over a very low heat until hot; or put into a
covered casserole with 1–2 tablespoons water. Heat very slowly, strain
away the surplus water and serve.

1 lb./½ kg. fresh peas or packet
   frozen peas
seasoning
4 rashers bacon

1 onion
½–1 oz./15–25 g. butter or
   margarine

To cook
1 Cook the shelled peas for 15–20 minutes in boiling, salted water, or the frozen peas for several minutes.
2 Strain and season well, then add the bacon, etc., fried while peas are cooking.
3 To cook the bacon, cut it into narrow strips and fry until crisp; when nearly ready add the finely sliced onion and butter or margarine and continue cooking until the onion is just tender, and separated into rings or pieces.
4 Heat the peas and bacon together for 1 minute.
5 Serve with meat or vegetable dishes, or as a light supper dish with fried eggs.

To freeze
See tips, opposite.

Freezing peas and other vegetables: You will find the method of blanching peas and other vegetables in your freezer instruction book. Blanching, i.e. partial cooking in boiling water for an average of 2 minutes (*but follow recommended time etc. in the book*), kills harmful enzymes that could cause the vegetables to lose colour, texture and flavour as well as making them deteriorate. The blanching process is the reason why frozen vegetables do not need as much cooking as fresh ones. Remember it is *not* worth your time and trouble freezing vegetables unless they are very fresh and you can buy them economically, or you grow them; it would be far better to bulk buy ready-frozen vegetables at a cheaper price than single small packets and use your freezer for other ways of saving time, trouble and money.

Spaghetti with meat sauce

☐ *Cooking time:* 1 hour   ☐ *Preparation time:* 30 minutes   ☐ *Main cooking utensils:* 2 saucepans   ☐ *Serves:* 4–5
☐ *Freezing tips:* either use a foil container, or if you want to put the sauce in a thick polythene bag, support the bag in a firm container (a sugar carton is ideal). Spoon in the sauce, allowing $\frac{1}{2}$ inch (1 cm.) headroom (see page 55). Freeze, then lift out the polythene bag – now a neat oblong for storage.   ☐ *Use within:* 2 months   ☐ *After freezing:* thaw sufficiently to heat through.

3 tablespoons olive oil
2 medium onions
2–3 cloves garlic
4 large tomatoes
1 medium aubergine
1 lb./½ kg. minced beef
2 tablespoons tomato purée
½ pint/3 dl. stock or water
¼ pint/1½ dl. red wine or use all
   stock

½ teaspoon powdered cinnamon
2 bay leaves
2 carrots
seasoning
8 oz./200 g. spaghetti
1 tablespoon oil
To serve
grated Kefalotyri*

* A very hard cheese made in Greece — Parmesan could be used.

To cook

1 Heat the olive oil. Fry the very finely chopped onions and crushed cloves of garlic (crush with salt on a board) for several minutes.
2 Add the skinned, chopped tomatoes and chopped aubergine.
3 Heat for 5 minutes with the onions; add the minced beef, stir this well with a fork to break up lumps.
4 Add the tomato purée, blended with stock, the wine, cinnamon, bay leaves, coarsely chopped or grated carrots and seasoning.
5 Simmer steadily for about 15 minutes. If necessary, remove the lid for the sauce to thicken towards the end of the cooking.
6 Meanwhile, boil the spaghetti in 4 pints (2¼ litres) boiling salted water; strain, arrange on dish and brush with oil. Pile the meat mixture on top and serve with cheese.

To freeze

Make the sauce, cool then freeze. This is the type of recipe where it is worthwhile preparing 3–4 times (or more) the quantity of sauce, then freezing this, for it can be used as a filling for pancakes, omelettes, etc., as well as with spaghetti or other pasta. You may care to freeze surplus spaghetti but I find it so easy to cook and it can lose some texture when frozen; however, see next pages (74 and 75).

Freezing garlic: Many people tell me they find garlic develops a funny, rather musty taste when frozen; personally I have not found this, but I do find it loses some of its potency.

Tagliatelle alla finanziera (pasta with chicken livers)

☐ *Cooking time:* 1¼ hours   ☐ *Preparation time:* 20 minutes   ☐ *Main cooking utensils:* 2 saucepans   ☐ *Serves:* 4
☐ *Freezing tips:* pack the pasta, see right, and sauce in separate containers. Page 72 suggests method of packing sauce, or it can be put into a foil container.   ☐ *Use within:* 2 months   ☐ *After freezing:* to reheat pasta, see right. The sauce should be thawed sufficiently to tip into a pan to be reheated, or heated in the foil container.

2 tablespoons oil
3 oz./75 g. butter
3 medium onions
4 large tomatoes
6 chicken livers or 12 oz./
300 g. diced rump steak*
1 pint/6 dl. chicken stock
seasoning
2 tablespoons concentrated
tomato purée

4 oz./100 g. mushrooms
¼ teaspoon each chopped thyme,
sage and parsley
½ pint/3 dl. red wine
6 oz./150 g. tagliatelle**
little chopped parsley and/or
chopped oregano
To serve
2–3 oz./50–75 g. Mozzarella or
Cheddar cheese, grated

* If using cheaper stewing meat, cook for a longer period.
** Other pasta could be used instead.

To cook

1 Heat the oil and half the butter; fry the fairly coarsely sliced onions in this, add the skinned, chopped tomatoes, chopped chicken livers or steak and cook for about 5 minutes.

2 Stir in the stock, seasoning, tomato purée and chopped mushrooms, together with the chopped herbs and wine.

3 Cook steadily for approximately 45 minutes–1 hour, until the sauce thickens.

4 Meanwhile cook the pasta in 3 pints (2 litres) boiling, salted water until just tender. Strain, toss in the remaining butter and chopped parsley and/or oregano (wild marjoram).

5 Arrange around the edge of a dish and fill the centre with the savoury mixture. Serve with grated cheese.

Freezing pasta: Filled pasta, such as cannelloni, are excellent stand-by meals. Cook, freeze, then reheat from the freezer. If you decide to freeze pasta such as used in this recipe, take care *not* to over-cook it. Rinse after cooking to get rid of surplus starch. Toss in melted butter or a little oil so the strands do not stick together, wrap and freeze. To reheat, tip into a generous amount of boiling, salted water. Heat for the minimum time only, then strain.

Hot trifle

☐ *Cooking time:* 30 minutes ☐ *Preparation time:* 15 minutes
☐ *Main cooking utensils:* 3 saucepans ☐ *Serves:* 4–6
☐ *Freezing tips:* keep in the dish and cover with foil or polythene.
☐ *Use within:* 1 week – 10 days ☐ *After freezing:* thaw out – this
takes 1–2 hours at room temperature, then warm gently.

1 plain sponge cake, or use a canned sponge pudding.
1 medium can apricots (or other fruit)
1¼ oz./ 35 g. custard powder

1 pint /6 dl. milk
1–2 oz./25–50 g. sugar
2 tablespoons sherry
1 oz./25 g. browned slivered almonds

To cook

1 Heat the sponge cake (wrap in foil and steam) or heat the canned pudding as directed on the can; heat the apricots.

2 While the pudding is heating make the custard. Blend the custard powder with a little cold milk, heat the rest of the milk. Pour over the blended custard powder, return to the pan with the sugar and cook, stirring, until smooth and thickened.

3 Slice the cake or pudding and put into a dish, moisten with a little of the hot fruit syrup; add the sherry and cover with most of the apricots, then the custard.

4 Decorate with slivered almonds and the remaining apricot halves.

5 Serve hot – put into a very low oven while serving the first course.

Variation: Use trifle sponge cake, split, fill with jam and moisten with fruit etc. as recipe. Allow the custard to cool, then decorate as above, adding whipped cream as well.

To freeze

This is the type of recipe that cannot be frozen for a long period but can be made ahead and frozen for a few days, for custard (as above) has a distinct tendency to curdle, but I find the thicker consistency generally used on a trifle is all right for this short time. It is worth doing if you have a busy period ahead or if by chance you have made a trifle and it has not been eaten.

Freezing egg custards: An ordinary egg and milk mixture can be frozen *without* cooking – a sensible thing to do if you are using up a lot of eggs and milk – but do not freeze a pudding, based on an egg custard, unless it has a very high percentage of thick (double) cream.

Use a frozen uncooked egg custard within 2 months. Cook in the usual way *without* defrosting, unless you have used an ovenproof container, in which case let it stand for a while at room temperature so the dish does not crack.

Coffee raisin pudding

☐ *Cooking time:* 1½ hours ☐ *Preparation time:* 20 minutes
☐ *Main cooking utensils:* fluted 1½–2-pint (1-litre) mould or basin;
steamer, saucepan, greaseproof paper or foil ☐ *Serves:* 6
☐ *Freezing tips:* either freeze, then remove the pudding from the basin
and wrap, or wrap the basin or mould, or use a foil-lined basin, foil or
polythene basin (the type suitable for heating *and* freezing). ☐ *Use
within:* cooked pudding – 3 months. Uncooked pudding – 1 month
☐ *After freezing:* no need to thaw out – steam for about 45 minutes if
ready-cooked, or 2¼ hours if frozen without cooking.

4 oz./100 g. butter
4 oz./100 g. castor sugar
2 eggs
6 oz./150 g. self-raising flour
(or plain flour and 1½ level
teaspoons baking powder)

3 oz./75 g. stoned raisins (or
chopped dates or mixed fruit)
3 tablespoons coffee essence
1 tablespoon milk

To cook

1 Cream together the butter and sugar until soft and light.
2 Gradually add the beaten eggs to the butter mixture – add a tablespoon of the sieved flour if the mixture appears to be curdling.
3 Fold in the remainder of the flour, or flour and baking powder, the raisins, coffee essence and milk. Turn into the prepared mould and cover with greaseproof paper or foil.
4 Steam over boiling water for 1½ hours.
5 Turn out on to hot dish and serve with fresh cream and a sprinkling of demerara sugar.

To freeze

You can freeze this pudding in two ways, i.e. you can make the pudding and freeze it without cooking, or you can cook the pudding as above, then cool and freeze.

Freezing sponge puddings: The recipe above is typical of the type of sponge pudding that freezes well. I generally make 2–3 times the normal quantity, cook enough for one meal and freeze the remainder in suitable containers. Remember to put the pudding back into the basin if you have removed this and to freeze without *any* cooking or to cook sponge puddings for the *complete* time, otherwise they will be heavy.

Apple charlotte

☐ *Cooking time:* 1 hour   ☐ *Preparation time:* 20 minutes   ☐ *Main cooking utensils:* 2-pint (generous 1-litre) pie dish, saucepan   ☐ *Oven temperature:* very moderate (325–350°F., 170–180°C., Gas Mark 3–4)
☐ *Serves:* 4–6
☐ *Freezing tips:* freeze before wrapping to prevent the crumbs adhering to the wrap, but wrap as soon as possible.   ☐ *Use within:* 5–6 months
☐ *After freezing:* unwrap and cook, or heat very slowly.

Crumb mixture
6 oz./150 g. fine white
    breadcrumbs
4 oz./100 g. chopped suet
2 oz./50 g. granulated or brown
    sugar
Fruit mixture
1 oz./25 g. butter
2 tablespoons water

1½ lb./¾ kg. cooking apples
2 oz./50 g. brown sugar
1 oz./25 g. sultanas or seedless
    raisins
¼ level teaspoon cinnamon or
    spice
Topping
1 oz./25 g. brown sugar
1 oz./25 g. butter

To cook

1 Mix the breadcrumbs, suet and granulated or brown sugar well together. Press three-quarters on to the bottom and sides of the pie dish.
2 Melt the butter in a pan, add the water, peeled, cored and diced apples and brown sugar. Cover. Heat gently, shaking and stirring occasionally, until the apples are well glazed but not too soft.
3 Remove from the heat and stir in the sultanas and cinnamon.
4 Pour into the prepared pie dish and top with the remaining crumb mixture, pressing down neatly. Wipe the edge of the dish. Sprinkle the crumbs with a layer of brown sugar and dot with butter.
5 Bake in the centre of the oven for about 40 minutes, until golden brown; this recipe is better baked more slowly than the Baked Rhubarb Betty, page 82.
6 Serve hot with cream or custard.

To freeze

This pudding, like the rhubarb Betty, freezes well, either when prepared or when cooked. Another useful way of using the freezer is to pack bags of crumbs that can be used in recipes such as this, or in stuffings, etc.

Freezing crumble: A crumble topping (made by rubbing 2 oz. (50 g.) margarine into 4 oz. (100 g.) flour, then adding 2–3 oz. (50–75 g.) sugar) is an excellent topping for fruit. Pre-cook fruit slightly if hard, then add crumble and bake as above. To freeze this, prepare ready for cooking and freeze, or cook until crumble is pale golden, cool then freeze. Use within 2 months.

Baked rhubarb Betty

☐ *Cooking time:* 40 minutes   ☐ *Preparation time:* 20 minutes
☐ *Main cooking utensils:* saucepan, 2-pint (generous 1-litre) pie dish or
ovenproof dish   ☐ *Oven temperature:* moderate (350–375°F., 180–
190°C., Gas Mark 4–5)   ☐ *Serves:* 4–5
☐ *Freezing tips:* freeze before wrapping to prevent the crumbs adhering
to the wrap, but wrap as soon as possible.   ☐ *Use within:* 5–6 months
☐ *After freezing:* unwrap and cook, or heat very slowly.

Crumb mixture
2 oz./50 g. butter
4 oz./100 g. brown or white
  sugar
6 oz./150 g. fairly coarse white
  breadcrumbs
grated rind of 1—2 oranges

½—1 teaspoon powdered cinnamon
Rhubarb mixture
1½ lb./¾ kg. rhubarb (weight
  after removing leaves)
juice of 2 oranges
3 oz./75 g. sugar

To cook

1 Melt the butter in a pan, then blend with the rest of the ingredients for the crumb mixture.
2 Cut the rhubarb into neat pieces and put half into the dish with half the orange juice and half the sugar.
3 Press half the crumb mixture on top of fruit, then cover with the rest of rhubarb, orange juice and sugar.
4 Press the rest of the crumb mixture over the top and bake in the centre of the oven until crisp and golden brown.
5 No sauce is necessary, as the rhubarb makes a good layer of juice, but it is excellent with orange-flavoured ice cream, or with thick cream or custard.

To freeze

You have a choice in this recipe. Either prepare pudding, but do not cook, then freeze it, or cook as above, cool, then freeze, or see page 81.

Freezing crumb puddings: This type of pudding freezes well; take particular care that the fruit mixture is not too moist, otherwise it can make the crumb mixture rather damp. If using similar dish to picture, thaw out first before cooking or heating, this takes 2—3 hours at room temperature. If you freeze the uncooked dessert in a flameproof dish use a low heat first to thaw out and heat the ingredients, *then* raise the heat to brown the crumbs.

Toffee fruit pudding

☐ *Cooking time:* minimum 2 hours ☐ *Preparation time:* 20 minutes
☐ *Main cooking utensils:* 2-pint (generous 1-litre) basin, foil or greased
paper to cover, steamer ☐ *Serves:* 6–7
☐ *Freezing tips:* cover and freeze in the basin; if you need the basin,
take out the frozen pudding and wrap, or line the basin with foil before
making the pudding, see page 49. ☐ *Use within:* 5 months
☐ *After freezing:* if you have frozen the pudding in the basin and it is
not metal or flameproof, allow to thaw out partially for 1–2 hours
before heating, so there is no fear of the basin cracking. To hasten this,
stand the basin in *cold* water after it has been at room temperature for
20–30 minutes.

1 oz./25 g. butter
1–2 oz./25–50 g. brown sugar
Crust
8 oz./200 g. self-raising flour
pinch salt
2 oz./50 g. very fine
   breadcrumbs

4 oz./100 g. shredded suet or
   melted butter
water to mix
Filling
1½–2 lb./¾–1 kg. fruit (see stage 4)
sugar to taste
little water, if necessary

To cook

1 Cover the bottom of the basin with most of the butter, use the rest to grease the sides lightly.

2 Sprinkle the sugar over the butter at the bottom of the basin.

3 Sieve the flour and salt. Add the crumbs, suet or melted and cooled butter and water to mix. Roll out and use two-thirds to line the basin.

4 Prepare the fruit: this pudding is delicious with a mixture of fruits as in the picture – peeled, sliced apples, gooseberries, greengages, cherries, strawberries or raspberries (canned or fresh). Fill the basin with the fruit.

5 Add sugar to taste and water, if necessary – do not use water with soft fruits.

6 Cover with a lid made from the remaining pastry. Seal the edges, and cover with greased foil or paper.

7 Steam over boiling water for at least 2 hours; fill up with boiling water as necessary,

8 Turn out and serve with cream or custard.

To freeze

Cook lightly if you intend to freeze the pudding. Allow the pudding to cool, then wrap, see left.

Freezing suet crust puddings: If your family like suet puddings as above, or a savoury such as steak and kidney pudding, make several at one time. I normally steam steak and kidney puddings for about 5 hours, but if I intend to freeze them I allow about 3 hours only, cool, then freeze. This means I can continue cooking the pudding and defrost it at the same time. The result is exactly as though freshly cooked.

Blintzes

☐ *Cooking time:* 15–20 minutes ☐ *Preparation time:* 10 minutes
☐ *Main cooking utensil:* frying pan ☐ *Serves:* 4
☐ *Freezing tips:* complete dish: make to stage 4 (see right-hand side),
cover then freeze. Pancakes: cook then freeze; if separated as suggested
on the right you always have pancakes ready to heat. ☐ *Use within:*
these particular filled pancakes – 4–6 weeks. Pancakes and filled
pancakes – 3 months, but the time varies with the filling. ☐ *After
freezing:* reheat filled pancakes slowly; defrost pancakes or reheat
frozen pancakes in little oil.

4 oz./100 g. plain flour
pinch salt
2 eggs
¼ pint/1½ dl. milk
1–2 teaspoons olive or corn
  oil (see below)*
Filling
8 oz./200 g. cottage cheese

3 level tablespoons castor sugar
few drops vanilla essence
To fry the pancakes
oil or fat
For the blintzes
butter
strawberry jam or redcurrant
  jelly

To cook

1 Sieve the flour and salt. Beat to a thick creamy batter with the eggs and milk.
2 Brush a thick frying pan with oil, or add a knob of fat. Heat, and fry the pancakes until golden brown on both sides. Keep hot.
3 Fill with the cottage cheese blended with the sugar and vanilla essence.
4 Fold up as an envelope, heat in the hot butter for a few minutes.
5 Serve topped with hot or cold jam, or cream if desired.

To freeze

Make the pancakes and fill, then fold (stage 4). Put into a foil container and cover. When ready to serve, pour over the melted butter, cover again and heat gently in the oven.

Freezing pancakes:* The batter is better if oil is added, as this prevents mixture being leathery after freezing. The batter above is thicker than usual; an ideal pancake batter for freezing is: 4 oz. (100 g.) flour, pinch salt, 2 eggs, ½ pint (3 dl.) milk, less 2 tablespoons and 2 teaspoons oil. Cook the pancakes and separate each one with oiled foil, polythene or greaseproof paper oiled on both sides. Wrap the parcel well. Peel off the number of pancakes required. Either defrost for about 1 hour, then fill and heat in an oiled pan, or in the oven; or heat the frozen pancakes in oil.

Some filled pancakes to freeze: Fill pancakes with cooked vegetable purées or cooked vegetables, fish or chicken in a white, brown or cheese sauce. Pour a little extra sauce into the container, *then* add the pancakes and coat with more sauce. By putting the sauce below as well as above the pancakes you prevent them drying when reheated.

Mince pies

□ *Cooking time:* see stage 4   □ *Preparation time:* mincemeat: 35–40 minutes; mince pies: depending on the pastry used   □ *Main cooking utensils:* deep patty tins, pastry cutters   □ *Makes:* 8–12 pies; $2\frac{1}{2}$ lb. ($1\frac{1}{4}$ kg.) mincemeat

□ *Freezing tips:* freeze in patty tins, remove and pack in polythene boxes, bags or foil.   □ *Use within:* cooked – 6 months; uncooked – 3–4 months   □ *After freezing:* if cooked – reheat gently, there is no need to defrost; if uncooked – put back into the patty tins while frozen, then thaw out for a short time so the pastry does not become too brown before it is cooked.

Mincemeat
1 apple
4 oz./100 g. shredded suet
4 oz./100 g. demerara sugar
finely grated rind of 1 lemon
juice of 1 lemon
1 lb./½ kg. mixed dried fruit
4 oz./100 g. mixed peel
4 oz./100 g. blanched almonds
½ teaspoon cinnamon
1 level teaspoon mixed spice
½ teaspoon grated nutmeg
4 tablespoons rum, brandy or
   whisky
Pastry
either shortcrust made with
   8 oz./200 g. flour, etc., or
flaky or puff pastry made with
   8 oz./200 g. flour, etc.
(see pages 91, 93)

To cook

1 To make the mincemeat, peel the apple, grate coarsely then mix with all the other ingredients. Put into clean jars and seal down.

2 To make the mince pies, roll out the pastry and cut rounds to fit into deep patty tins; put in the mincemeat.

3 Cover with the smaller rounds of pastry. Brush the edges with water and seal together. It is usual to make slits on top to allow steam to escape, but this is not essential.

4 Bake in the centre of the oven as follows: shortcrust pastry – approximately 20 minutes in the centre of a hot oven, 425–450°F., 220–230°C., Gas Mark 7–8, lowering heat slightly after 10–15 minutes. Flaky pastry – 20 minutes in the centre of a very hot oven, 450–475°F., 230–240°C., Gas Mark 8–9, reducing the heat slightly after 10 minutes if necessary. Puff pastry – 15 minutes in the centre of a very hot oven, 475°F., 240°C., Gas Mark 9, reducing the heat after 10 minutes.

5 Serve hot or cold. They may be dusted with castor or icing sugar.

To freeze

Mincemeat does not need freezing; it stores well in an ordinary cupboard, but mince pies freeze well and save one task at Christmas time. See comments on pastry in the freezer on the next few pages.

Chausson aux cerises (cherry turnover)

□ *Cooking time:* 35–40 minutes   □ *Preparation time:* 35 minutes, plus time for pastry to stand   □ *Main cooking utensils:* pie plate, flat baking sheet   □ *Oven temperature:* hot to very hot (450–475°F., 230–240°C., Gas Mark 8–9) then moderate (375°F., 190°C., Gas Mark 5)
□ *Serves:* 4–5
□ *Freezing tips:* freeze on the pie plate or tin. If this is foil there is no need to remove the pie. If it is a dish you will need again, remove the pie and wrap.   □ *Use within:* 4 months   □ *After freezing:* put back on to the pie plate or tin. If cooked, heat gently; if uncooked, thaw out for about 1 hour, then cook as the recipe.

90

Puff pastry
8 oz./200 g. flour, preferably
  plain
pinch salt
½–1 tablespoon lemon juice
cold water
8 oz./200 g. butter
Filling
1 lb./½ kg. black or red or
  Morello (cooking) cherries
2–4 oz./50–100 g. sugar
  (depending upon type of
  cherries)
2 oz./50 g. blanched almonds
water or white wine
Glaze
milk or beaten egg

To cook

1 Sieve the flour and salt. Add the lemon juice and ice cold water to make a rolling consistency.

2 Roll out to a neat oblong, put the butter in the centre and fold the dough to cover. Turn the pastry at right angles, seal ends and rib (i.e. depress with rolling pin at regular intervals).

3 Re-roll to an oblong, gently and lightly; fold, etc. Continue like this until the pastry has had seven foldings and seven rollings. Flour lightly and put into a cool place between rollings.

4 Finally roll out the pastry and make two equal-sized rounds.

5 Put one round on to a baking sheet. Cover with the cherries, sugar, almonds and sprinkling of water or wine. Brush the edges with water. Cover with the second round of pastry. Seal the edges, score the pastry to make a pattern and glaze with milk or beaten egg.

6 Bake in the centre of the oven until crisp and golden brown, reducing the heat after 20 minutes. Serve hot with cream.

To freeze

As there is a tendency for the bottom pastry to become a little soft with freezing and cooking, be very sparing with the liquid in the filling. You can also sprinkle the bottom layer of pastry with a little flour, cornflour or semolina and sugar before adding the fruit. Either prepare then freeze, or cook as above, cool and freeze.

Apple tart

☐ *Cooking time:* 45 minutes   ☐ *Preparation time:* 25 minutes
☐ *Main cooking utensil:* 8-inch (20-cm.) pie plate   ☐ *Oven temperature:* hot (425°F., 220°C., Gas Mark 7), then moderate (350–375°F., 180–190°C., Gas Mark 4–5)   ☐ *Serves:* 4–6
☐ *Freezing tips:* freeze on the pie plate or tin. If this is foil there is no need to remove the pie. If using a dish you will need again, remove pie and wrap.   ☐ *Use within:* 4 months   ☐ *After freezing:* put back on to the pie plate or tin. If cooked, heat gently; if uncooked, thaw out for about 1 hour, then cook as the recipe.

Shortcrust pastry
8 oz./200 g. flour, preferably plain
pinch salt
4 oz./100 g. fat

water to mix
Filling
1½ lb./¾ kg. cooking apples
4 oz./100 g. castor sugar
icing or castor sugar

To cook

1 Sieve the flour and salt into bowl and rub in the fat until the mixture resembles fine breadcrumbs. Mix to a dough with water.
2 Turn out on to a floured board and knead lightly. Divide in two and roll each piece into a circle slightly larger than the plate. Line the plate with one piece of pastry.
3 Put the peeled, sliced apples on to the pastry; add the sugar. Cover with the second piece of pastry and trim and decorate edges. (See points made under To freeze, page 91.)
4 Bake in the centre of the oven for 15 minutes at the higher temperature, then lower the heat for 30 minutes. Dust with sugar.

To freeze

See the recipe on page 91, and ways to freeze pastry, page 94.

Freezing fruit: If you grow fruit or can obtain really fresh fruit economically, I would certainly freeze the surplus.

Soft fruits — raspberries, loganberries, blackberries, etc.: do not wash if possible; pack small quantities in containers, add sugar between each layer if desired, although I prefer to freeze *without* sugar. Blackcurrants should be topped and tailed.

Strawberries: always slightly disappointing — freeze on flat trays, pack when firm. Use soft fruits within 8 months.

Hard fruits — apricots, plums, damsons, etc.: nicest if *lightly* cooked in sugar syrup. Large fruit can be halved, apples and rhubarb can be sliced or cut in pieces, cooked for 1—2 minutes only in boiling water, drained then packed. Add a little lemon to keep apples white and drop into the boiling water *as you peel them*, or keep in weak brine (1 tablespoon kitchen salt to 2 pints (generous litre) water). Skinned sliced peaches and pears can be frozen in lemon-flavoured syrup (without cooking) — make sure you are generous with the syrup.

Freeze fruit purées for use in sauces, tarts, cold fruit moulds, etc. Allow ½ inch (1 cm.) headroom when packing fruit in syrup or with purée. Use hard fruits and purées within 8—9 months (melon within 3 months). See page 15 for citrus fruit.

Puff pastry desserts

Each recipe on the right is based on 8 oz. (200 g.) frozen puff pastry or pastry made with 4 oz. (100 g.) plain flour, etc. — see method, page 91. Allow frozen pastry to defrost slightly before rolling out.

Ways to freeze pastry: Pastry may be prepared, formed into neat shapes of convenient weight, then wrapped. If you do not want to make your own pastry for the freezer you can buy commercially made and frozen dough. When you label the pastry I would also add weight of the dough so you know which package to choose for a certain dish.

Pies, tarts, etc. may be made and frozen ready for cooking later. If you make vol-au-vent cases, freeze on flat baking sheets

before wrapping, so you do not spoil the shape. Wrap when hard. Sweet and savoury pies, tarts, flans may be cooked in the usual way, cooled then frozen. I would use foil dishes where possible.

Rounds, squares or other shapes of pastry may also be frozen. These can be uncooked, or cooked and cooled then frozen. Separate each round, etc. with foil or polythene so you can remove these easily.

Caramelled palmiers

Sprinkle the pastry board with sugar, roll pastry to a neat oblong. Roll one long side as for a Swiss roll but stop at the centre. Roll the other side in the same way so the two rolls meet in the centre. Cut into slices $\frac{1}{4}$—$\frac{1}{3}$ inch (good $\frac{1}{2}$ cm.) thick and press each slice in sugar. Bake for 5–6 minutes, above the centre, in a hot to very hot oven (425–450°F., 220–230°C., Gas Mark 7–8); turn over, bake for another 5–6 minutes. Serve with ice cream, or sandwich two with cream. Makes about 10–12.

To freeze: Prepare as above, then cool. I prefer to freeze this particular recipe without the filling. Thaw out; the pastry should still be crisp but is improved by being warmed for 2–3 minutes in the oven. Use within 4 months.

Lemon mille feuilles

Roll out the pastry thinly and cut into two equal-sized squares, about 6–7 inches (15–18 cm.). Put on to a baking sheet and cook for 15 minutes in a hot to very hot oven; reduce the heat after 10 minutes if becoming too brown. When cold, spread one square with lemon curd and top with $\frac{1}{4}$ pint ($1\frac{1}{2}$ dl.) whipped cream, flavoured with a little grated lemon rind. Top with the second square. Blend 6 oz. (150 g.) sieved icing sugar with lemon juice to give a spreading consistency. Take out 2 tablespoons icing and add 2 tablespoons cocoa. Spread lemon icing over the pastry, do not allow to dry. Make lines of the chocolate icing with a No. 1 writing pipe and drag the back of a knife towards and away from you across the lines, to give a feathering effect. Serves 6–8.

To freeze: Either freeze the two squares of raw or baked pastry (use uncooked pastry within 1 month, cooked pastry within 4 months) or prepare dessert as above and freeze. Thaw out at room temperature, this takes 2–3 hours, then serve at once so the pastry is not softened by the cream.

Ice cream flan

☐ *Cooking time:* 20–25 minutes ☐ *Preparation time:* 15–20 minutes
☐ *Main cooking utensils:* 8-inch (20-cm.) fluted flan ring or tin on
baking sheet ☐ *Oven temperature:* moderately hot (400°F., 200°C.,
Gas Mark 5–6) ☐ *Serves:* 6–8
☐ *Freezing tips:* freeze in the flan ring or tin. Wrap very carefully or
store in a polythene box so the fragile pastry does not break. ☐ *Use
within:* flan – 6 months; ice cream – 2–3 months ☐ *After freezing:*
allow the flan to thaw out; this takes about 2 hours at room
temperature.

Rich sweet pastry
4 oz./100 g. margarine or butter
1–2 oz./25–50 g. sugar
6 oz./150 g. plain flour
1 oz./25 g. cornflour
egg yolk

little water, if necessary
Filling
canned, frozen or fresh fruit
2 blocks ice cream, or home made
   ice cream (see page 102)

To cook

1 Cream the margarine or butter with the sugar until soft and light.
2 Work in the flour and cornflour, then add the egg yolk and enough water to give a rolling consistency.
3 Knead lightly until smooth. Roll out and line the flan ring, which should stand on a baking sheet.
4 Bake blind until crisp and golden brown. Allow to cool.
5 Fill with well drained fruit and spoonfuls of ice cream.
6 Serve fairly soon after filling, although this is nicer if the ice cream softens very slightly.

To freeze

Although cooked flans store well in tins, they store even better in the freezer. Bake, do not over-brown, in case you want to add a filling and heat. In this recipe freeze the flan in one container and the ice cream separately. Do not put together until almost ready to serve.

97

Ham and pork rolls

□ *Cooking time:* 20 minutes   □ *Preparation time:* 40 minutes, plus time for pastry to stand   □ *Main cooking utensils:* flat baking tray or baking sheet   □ *Oven temperature:* very hot (475°F., 240°C., Gas Mark 9)   □ *Makes:* 18 rolls
□ *Freezing tips:* freeze on flat baking trays, then pack.   □ *Use within:* 3–4 months   □ *After freezing:* put back on flat trays and reheat or cook from the frozen state.

Puff pastry
8 oz./200 g. plain flour
pinch salt
squeeze lemon juice
water
8 oz./200 g. butter, preferably
  unsalted

Filling
12-oz./300-g. can chopped ham
  and pork
Glaze
1 egg

To cook

1 Sieve the flour and salt into a bowl.

2 Mix with the lemon juice and water to an elastic dough; roll out to an oblong.

3 Put the butter in the centre of the dough, then fold the bottom third over this, then bring down the top third.

4 Turn the pastry, seal the ends and roll out to an oblong again. Repeat until the pastry has had seven rollings and seven foldings; put in a cold place for 10–15 minutes in between each rolling to keep it firm.

5 Cut the ham and pork into fingers, about $\frac{3}{4}$ inch (1$\frac{1}{2}$ cm.) wide.

6 Roll out the pastry to a strip about 2 inches (5 cm.) wide.

7 Put the filling along the pastry, then brush the edges of the pastry with egg and fold over to enclose the meat. Seal the edges firmly, cut into individual portions and make two slits on the top of each. Brush with egg.

8 Bake for the time and temperature given until crisp and golden brown, reducing the heat if necessary. Serve cold with salad.

To freeze

I think this kind of savoury dish or similar recipes, e.g. sausage rolls, are most useful to store in the freezer. I prefer freezing the uncooked rolls so the filling does not dry.

Fiesta pie

□ *Cooking time:* 30–35 minutes   □ *Preparation time:* 25 minutes
□ *Main cooking utensils:* 8-inch (20-cm.) flan ring and baking sheet or
tin   □ *Oven temperature:* see stages 4 and 7   □ *Serves:* 4–6
□ *Freezing tips:* freeze in the flan ring or sandwich tin then remove
and wrap; or freeze in a shallow flameproof dish (if you can spare this),
then reheat in the same dish.   □ *Use within:* 4 months   □ *After
freezing:* heat through slowly without defrosting.

6 oz./150 g. flour, preferably plain
seasoning (see stage 1)
3 oz./75 g. butter
2 oz./50 g. Cheddar cheese
approximately 1½ tablespoons
  water
Filling
3 eggs
1 small onion or shallot

1 oz./25 g. butter
4 oz./100 g. shelled prawns
¼ pint/1½ dl. thin (single)
  cream
½ tablespoon made mustard
2 tomatoes, thinly sliced
Garnish
fennel or parsley
prawn heads

To cook

1 Sieve together the flour, salt and 1 level teaspoon dry mustard. Rub in the butter until the mixture resembles fine breadcrumbs.
2 Add the grated cheese and bind together with water to form a firm dough.
3 Put the flan ring on an upturned baking sheet or tin (or use a sandwich tin or ovenproof dish).
4 Line the flan ring with the pastry. Flute the edges and prick the base; chill. Bake blind* in a hot oven, 425–450°F., 220–230°C., Gas Mark 7–8, for 15 minutes.
5 Remove the foil or greaseproof paper, etc., put in the filling.
6 To make the filling, beat the eggs, fry the chopped onion or shallot in hot butter and add to the eggs with all the ingredients except the tomatoes. Arrange the sliced tomatoes on top of the filling in the flan case.
7 Bake for about 15–20 minutes in a moderate oven, 350–375°F., 180–190°C., Gas Mark 4–5, until the custard has set.
8 Serve cold, garnished with fennel or parsley and prawn heads.
*To bake blind, cover the pastry with greaseproof paper or foil, then beans or crusts of bread.

Variations: Omit the fried onion, add 2–3 oz. (50–75 g.) grated cheese and reduce the amount of mustard. Omit the prawns and fried onion, add 2–3 oz. (50–75 g.) grated cheese and 2–3 rashers chopped bacon. For a deeper flan use double the amount of cream, or use half cream and half milk.

To freeze

Cook as above to end of stage 7. Cool then freeze. The filling freezes extremely well as it has a certain amount of cream, so it gives a richer flavour and good texture to the custard mixture.

This recipe is one example of a quiche, but all quiche fillings using *all* cream or half cream and half milk can be frozen.

Cherry vanilla ice

☐ *Freezing time:* 1½–2 hours   ☐ *Preparation time:* 20 minutes
☐ *Main utensil:* freezing tray   ☐ *Serves:* 6
☐ *Freezing tips:* you may find it easier to freeze to stage 6 (until half-set) in the freezing compartment of your refrigerator, especially if your freezer is situated in the garage or outside the kitchen.   ☐ *Use within:* 3 months   ☐ *After freezing:* allow the ice cream to stand in the kitchen for about 15–20 minutes before serving so it is not too hard.

3 oz./75 g. glacé cherries	2–3 oz./50–75 g. icing sugar,*
1–2 oz./25–50 g. angelica	sieved
2 eggs	½ pint/3 dl. thick (double) cream
¼ teaspoon vanilla essence	¼ pint/1½ dl. thin (single) cream

*Do not exceed this amount otherwise the ice cream does not freeze well.

To prepare

1 Chop the glacé cherries and angelica into small pieces; if the angelica is very hard and sugary rinse it quickly in warm water, then dry thoroughly.

2 Put the eggs, vanilla essence and sugar into a basin and whisk until thick – you should be able to see the mark of the whisk. Add the cherries and angelica.

3 Whip the thick cream until it holds a shape.

4 Gradually whisk the thin cream into the thick cream.

5 Fold *half* the cream into the *thick* egg mixture and spoon into the freezing tray or any other suitable container.

6 Freeze until half-set, remove, beat and fold in the remainder of of the cream. Continue freezing until firm in the freezing compartment of the refrigerator, or in your freezer.

Freezing ice creams: As you know, the food to be frozen in a home freezer must be frozen in the coldest position or at the coldest setting (follow the instructions given in the manufacturers' book or instruction manual), but ice cream may be frozen in any position in the freezer. Cover the container and seal firmly. See also page 104.

Contents	Date in	No of Packs	Position
Chicken	2·Nov	111	Shelf 2
Ice Cream	4·Nov	1	" 1
Bread	10·Dec	111111	Shelf 2
Ham + Pork rolls	10·Dec	111	" 3

Marshmallow ice cream

☐ *Cooking time:* few minutes   ☐ *Freezing time:* 1½–2 hours
☐ *Preparation:* 15 minutes   ☐ *Main cooking utensils:* saucepan*,
freezing tray   ☐ *Serves:* 6–8
☐ *Freezing tips:* I like to freeze ice cream in a fairly deep container so
that I can scoop out attractive rounds of ice cream as shown in the
picture.   ☐ *Use within:* 3 months, but see on the right   ☐ *After
freezing:* this particular ice cream softens very quickly, so take it out of
the freezer only 5–10 minutes before required.

4 oz./100 g. white marshmallows**	1 oz./25 g. icing sugar, sieved
¼ pint/1½ dl. milk	scant 1 teaspoon vanilla essence
2 eggs	½ pint/3 dl. thick (double) cream

*Use a strong pan so that mixture cannot burn.
**To cut marshmallows use kitchen scissors dipped in very hot water.

To prepare
1 Halve 3 oz. (75 g.) of the marshmallows and put into a saucepan with the milk.
2 Heat gently until the marshmallows are nearly melted. Remove from the heat and leave to cool; the marshmallows will continue melting for a few minutes in the pan.
3 Whisk the eggs, sugar and essence until thick and fluffy.
4 Whip the cream until it holds its shape.
5 Gradually blend with the whisked egg mixture and the melted marshmallows.
6 Chop the remaining 1 oz. (25 g.) marshmallows very finely and fold into the mixture.
7 Pour into the freezing tray and freeze until firm in the freezing compartment of the refrigerator, or in your freezer.

Variations: Add chopped glacé pineapple or chopped nuts, or well drained canned pineapple pieces at stage 6. Serve with mocha sauce made by heating 6 oz. (150 g.) plain chocolate with ¼ pint (1½ dl.) weak black coffee. Cool before serving.

To freeze
See comments in the previous recipe. If you intend to store this ice cream for the full 3 months in your freezer I would omit the chopped marshmallows, which tend to become a little leathery after 3—4 weeks.

Sunrise sorbet

□ *Cooking time:* few minutes extra beating during freezing saucepan □ *Serves:* 6–8

□ *Preparation time:* 10 minutes, plus □ *Main utensils:* 2 freezing trays,

□ *Freezing tips:* if you intend to store sorbets in your freezer, use gelatine to prevent ice crystals forming, see right. □ *Use within:* 4 months □ *After freezing:* sorbets tend to be rather firm in texture when they come out of the freezer; leave them at room temperature for 10–15 minutes before serving.

6 oz./150 g. granulated sugar	4 tablespoons rose hip syrup
¾ pint/4½ dl. water	1 egg white
juice of ½ lemon	1 oz./25 g. castor sugar
grated rind and juice of 1 medium orange	

To prepare

1 This may be frozen with the refrigerator at normal setting or in *any* position in the home freezer, not necessarily in the coldest position or with the temperature reduced to coldest setting.
2 Dissolve the sugar over a gentle heat in ¼ pint (1½ dl.) water.
3 Remove from the heat and add the rest of the water, the fruit juices, orange rind and rose hip syrup.
4 Stir well then pour into two freezing trays.
5 Put into the freezing compartment of the refrigerator, or freezer, and chill for 1 hour.
6 Turn into a bowl; whisk the egg white with castor sugar until stiff; mix with the rose hip mixture.
7 Chill for a further 45 minutes and re-whisk.
8 Pour back into the trays and chill for 1½–2 hours, or until firm.
9 Spoon into small dishes or sundae glasses.

To freeze for storing

Soften 2 teaspoons gelatine in 2 tablespoons of the water from the recipe above, then dissolve in the hot sugar and water (stage 2).

Freezing sorbets: A sorbet is a most refreshing dessert. The recipe above can be adapted to give other flavours, e.g. use ¾ pint (4½ dl.) plus 4 tablespoons thin fruit purée instead of the water and rose hip syrup. For a lighter texture increase the egg whites to 2–3.

Fruit bannock

□ *Cooking time:* 15–20 minutes   □ *Preparation time:* 25 minutes,
plus time for dough to prove, etc.   □ *Main cooking utensil:* flat baking
tray or sheet   □ *Oven temperature:* moderately hot (400°F., 200°C.,
Gas Mark 5–6)   □ *Makes:* 8 portions
□ *Freezing tips:* wrap in thick foil or polythene, or put into a polythene
container.   □ *Use within:* 6 weeks   □ *After freezing:* thaw out (at
room temperature this takes about 1 hour), or wrap in foil, to prevent
the outside becoming too brown before hot in the centre, and heat for 15
minutes in a moderate to moderately hot oven.

Yeast batter
2 oz./50 g. plain flour*
1 oz./25 g. butter or lard, melted
4 tablespoons warm milk
¼ oz./10 g. fresh yeast or
   ½ teaspoon dried yeast
Additional ingredients
6 oz./150 g. plain flour*

1 oz./25 g. castor sugar
4 tablespoons warm milk
1 oz./25 g. sultanas
1 oz./25 g. currants
½ oz./15 g. chopped candied peel
Glaze
milk

*Preferably strong.

To cook
1 Blend the batter ingredients together in a mixing bowl and leave for 20–30 minutes, until frothy.
2 Add the additional ingredients and mix well. Knead the dough thoroughly.
3 Put the dough to prove in a greased polythene bag or covered bowl until double in size – about 1 hour.
4 Knead the dough until smooth and shape into a ball. Flatten to approximately 8 inches (20 cm.) across and ½ inch (1 cm.) thick.
5 Put on a greased and floured tray and slash with sharp knife into eight sections. Brush the top with milk.
6 Cover with greased polythene if possible. Prove for about 30 minutes.
7 Brush the top again with milk. Bake for the time and temperature given, until firm to the touch. Split and serve with butter.

To freeze
Make quite certain that the bannock is cold, then wrap and freeze.

Freezing fresh yeast: It is not always possible to obtain fresh yeast when needed, so freeze a supply. Divide this into useful-sized quantities. Wrap and store. Yeast keeps for a year in the freezer. When you require this, either grate it while still frozen, or allow to thaw out – a 1-oz. (25-g.) piece of yeast will be soft enough to use after about 30 minutes at room temperature.

Cheese caraway bread

☐ *Cooking time:* 30–40 minutes   ☐ *Preparation time:* 25 minutes, plus time for dough to prove, etc.   ☐ *Main cooking utensils:* two 1-lb. (½-kg.) loaf tins   ☐ *Oven temperature:* hot (425–450°F., 220–230°C., Gas Mark 7–8)   ☐ *Makes:* 2 small loaves
☐ *Freezing tips:* bread is extremely versatile in the ways in which it can be frozen: either bake and freeze as in this recipe; or prepare the dough, and freeze, then bake it later (see page 113).   ☐ *Use within:* 6 weeks   ☐ *After freezing:* thaw out at room temperature, or warm (see page 108).

1 oz./25 g. fresh yeast
1 teaspoon sugar
½ pint/3 dl. warm milk
1 lb./½ kg. plain flour
1 level teaspoon salt
2 eggs

8 oz./200 g. Cheddar cheese,
   grated
1 oz./25 g. caraway seeds
Glaze
little melted butter

To cook

1 Cream the yeast and sugar together and add the warm liquid.
2 Sieve the flour and salt. Make a well in the centre, put in the yeast liquid and sprinkle the flour lightly over the top.
3 Leave in warm place until the surface is covered with small bubbles, i.e. the sponge breaks through; this takes about 15 minutes.
4 Mix with the flour; add the eggs, cheese and caraway seeds.
5 Knead thoroughly, then put into a bowl, cover with a clean cloth, or put into a large greased polythene bag.
6 Allow to prove until double in size.
7 Knock back and knead until smooth.
8 Divide the dough into two portions and shape into tin loaves.
9 Put into warmed greased tins, brush the tops of the loaves with melted butter. Allow to prove again, until the dough has risen to tops of tins.
10 Bake for the time and temperature given.
11 Serve for a main meal with soup, or with fillings for sandwiches.

To freeze

Cool after baking, then wrap and freeze.

Freezing bread: Home-made bread of all kinds can be frozen. Use within 6 weeks. Either thaw out at room temperature for about 2 hours or heat loaf, wrapped in foil, for 30–40 minutes in a moderate to moderately hot oven. It is worth buying sliced bread or slicing some of your own, for slices of frozen bread can be toasted without thawing.

Croissants

□ *Cooking time:* 15–20 minutes   □ *Preparation time:* 40 minutes, plus time for dough to stand and prove, etc.   □ *Main cooking utensil:* flat baking tray or sheet   □ *Oven temperature:* hot (425–450°F., 220–230°C., Gas Mark 7–8)   □ *Makes:* 12 portions
□ *Freezing tips:* pack carefully before freezing so the shape and crust is not spoiled.   □ *Use within:* 6–8 weeks   □ *After freezing:* heat through in the oven; allow 10 minutes if unwrapped, or 15 minutes if wrapped in foil, in a moderate oven (the latter gives a softer crust to the croissants).

1 teaspoon sugar
½ pint/3 dl., less 4 tablespoons,
    warm water
1 oz./25 g. fresh yeast or
    1 level tablespoon dried yeast
1 lb./½ kg. plain flour

1–2 level teaspoons salt
1 oz./25 g. lard or butter
1 egg
4 oz./100 g. margarine or butter
Glaze
beaten egg

To cook

1 Prepare the yeast liquid as page 111.

2 Sieve the flour and salt. Rub in the lard or butter, then add the yeast liquid and egg. Knead until the dough is very smooth.

3 Roll the dough into a long strip about 20 inches (50 cm.) by 6 inches (15 cm.) by ¼ inch (½ cm.) thick.

4 Divide the margarine or butter into three, then cover two-thirds of the dough with one part of the margarine or butter.

5 Fold in three; bring the plain part up first and the bottom part down, so the dough is like a closed envelope.

6 Turn at right angles and seal the ends. Roll and repeat twice with the rest of the margarine or butter – put away in a cool place for 10 minutes, then roll and fold three times more.

7 Leave in a cool place for 1 hour, then roll out to an oblong shape and cut into 12 triangles.

8 To shape the croissants, twist the triangles loosely towards the point and form into a crescent. Put on a baking tray and glaze.

9 Allow to prove for 30 minutes, until double size then bake for the time and temperature given. Serve very fresh or hot.

To freeze

Either freeze on flat trays then pack, or pack carefully, so you do not damage the shape, and freeze.

Freezing uncooked dough: If you prefer to freeze the croissants, or any yeast dough before baking, increase the amount of yeast by 50%. Either prepare the dough until kneaded, but not risen (proven), then pack in well greased polythene bags, seal and freeze at once; or prepare dough, knead, allow to prove, then knead again. Put into the well greased polythene bags, seal and freeze at once. Emphasis is given on quick freezing to prevent dough rising in the bags. Use within 6 weeks if a rich dough (as this recipe) or 2 months if a plain bread. Take the bag out of the freezer, open seal and leave for 4–5 hours at room temperature or about 12 hours in the refrigerator then continue as the recipe.

Hot cross buns

□ *Cooking time:* 10 minutes   □ *Preparation time:* 15 minutes, plus time for dough to prove   □ *Main cooking utensil:* flat baking tray or sheet   □ *Oven temperature:* very hot (450–475°F., 230–240°C., Gas Mark 8–9)   □ *Makes:* 12 buns
□ *Freezing tips:* wrap, or put into polythene containers. Do not handle too roughly while fresh otherwise you will spoil the shape.   □ *Use within:* 6 weeks   □ *After freezing:* take from the freezer and heat slowly for 15–20 minutes, or wrap in foil and heat for 15 minutes in a moderately hot oven.

½ oz./15 g. yeast
1 teaspoon sugar
approximately 12 tablespoons
    warm water, milk and water
    or milk
12 oz./300 g. plain flour
good pinch salt
1 oz./25 g. margarine
1 oz./25 g. sugar
4–6 oz./100–150 g. dried fruit

3–4 oz./75–100 g. candied peel
1 teaspoon spice
Shortcrust pastry
2 oz./50 g. flour
pinch salt
1 oz./25 g. fat
1 dessertspoon water
Glaze
2 tablespoons sugar
2 tablespoons water

To cook

1 Prepare the yeast liquid as page 111.
2 Sieve the flour and salt into a warm bowl. Rub in the margarine, add the sugar, fruit, peel and spice.
3 When the yeast liquid is ready, work in and knead thoroughly.
4 Put in a warm place for approximately 1 hour to prove, i.e. until the dough doubles in size.
5 Form into round buns and prove for 15 minutes on a warm baking tray.
6 Make the shortcrust pastry by sieving the flour and salt, rubbing in the fat until the mixture resembles fine breadcrumbs and mixing to a stiff dough with a little water. Cut into thin strips and arrange in the form of a cross on top of the buns.
7 Bake for the time and temperature given until firm to the touch.
8 Mix the sugar with the water.
9 Immediately the buns come from the oven, brush the tops with this glaze.

To freeze

So often holiday periods mean a great deal of extra cooking and little leisure for the housewife. By planning ahead you can prepare so many special dishes for busy times of the year. These hot cross buns will taste just as good when baked and frozen as they will when freshly cooked.

Cheese and bacon scones

☐ *Cooking time:* 12–15 minutes ☐ *Preparation time:* 10 minutes
☐ *Main cooking utensils:* 2-inch (5-cm.) pastry cutter, flat baking tray
or sheet ☐ *Oven temperature:* hot (425°F., 220°C., Gas Mark 7)
☐ *Makes:* 12–14 scones
☐ *Freezing tips:* cool, then pack and freeze. I use polythene boxes so I
can remove the number of scones required with the minimum of
trouble. ☐ *Use within:* 3 months ☐ *After freezing:* warm through
for a few minutes in a moderately hot oven.

8 oz./200 g. self-raising flour
2 level teaspoons baking powder
½ level teaspoon dry mustard
¼ level teaspoon salt
pinch pepper
2 oz./50 g. margarine

3 oz./75 g. cheese, finely grated
3 rashers bacon, cooked and
  finely chopped
6–7 tablespoons milk
Glaze
egg yolk

To cook
1 Sieve the flour, baking powder, mustard, salt and pepper together.
2 Place all the ingredients in a bowl. Mix together thoroughly with a wooden spoon to form a dough.
3 Turn out on to a lightly floured board.
4 Roll out to ½-inch (1-cm.) thickness. Cut into rounds.
5 Place on a baking tray and brush the tops with egg yolk.
6 Bake for the time and temperature given.
7 Cool on a wire tray.
8 To serve, split and top with butter.

To freeze
Cool thoroughly, then pack and freeze.

Freezing scones and baking powder breads: I always make rather large batches of scones and various kinds of bread without yeast and freeze the surplus. Plain scones and baking powder breads or those containing dried fruit can be stored for up to 6 months in the freezer.

36 Cheese and bacon scones use by end Sept.

Strawberry hazelnut gâteau

□ *Cooking time:* 15 minutes   □ *Preparation time:* 25 minutes
□ *Main cooking utensils:* two 8- to 9-inch (20- to 23-cm.) sandwich
tins   □ *Oven temperature:* moderate (350–375°F., 180–190°C., Gas
Mark 4–5)   □ *Serves:* 6–8
□ *Freezing tips:* although this gâteau looks so delicate, it will be quite
hard and firm when frozen so can be wrapped in foil or polythene, or
put into a polythene container.   *Use within:* 3 months   □ *After
freezing:* unwrap the gâteau as soon as you remove it from the freezer.
This prevents the wrapping sticking to the cream, etc. This takes about
3–4 hours, at room temperature, to thaw out.

Cakes
4 large eggs
5 oz./125 g. castor sugar
2 oz./50 g. self-raising flour,
   or plain flour and $\frac{1}{2}$ teaspoon
   baking powder
2 oz./50 g. hazelnuts, ground or
   finely chopped

Filling and topping
$\frac{1}{2}$ pint/3 dl. thick cream
1 tablespoon brandy
1–2 tablespoons sugar
2 oz./50 g. hazelnuts
1 lb./$\frac{1}{2}$ kg. strawberries

To cook

1 Grease and flour the sandwich tins or line the bottoms with greased greaseproof paper.
2 Whisk the eggs and sugar until thick. Fold in the sieved flour or flour and baking powder and the hazelnuts.
3 Pour into the tins. Bake for approximately 15 minutes in a moderate oven until just firm to the touch; do not over-cook.
4 Turn out and allow to cool.
5 Whip the cream, add the brandy and sugar gradually.
6 Spread just under half the cream over one sponge, then top with half the hazelnuts, chopped coarsely, and a thick layer of sliced strawberries.
7 Put the second sponge on top and spread with a little cream.
8 Arrange the whole strawberries on top and pipe a narrow border of cream around the edge. Decorate with whole hazelnuts.
9 Serve as a dessert or cake.

To freeze

This type of decorated cake can be damaged during freezing unless you use great care. Do not wrap before freezing. I find it easiest if I freeze on a cake board or strong plate then wrap in polythene and put the gâteau into a large polythene box. Allow time to thaw out. I think a little softening of the filling etc. is good, as it gives a moist texture to the cake.

Freezing layer cakes: Freeze as above with fillings, or freeze each half of the sponge; separate with waxed paper, polythene or foil, then freeze and wrap. If you wrap too soon, the wrap does stick to the delicate outside of a sponge. Use within 6 months. Butter icings and fillings can be frozen in separate containers. Use within 3 months.

Gâteau mont blanc

☐ *Cooking time:* 30–35 minutes   ☐ *Preparation time:* 40–45 minutes
☐ *Main cooking utensils:* 8- to 9-inch (20- to 23-cm.) sandwich tin
☐ *Oven temperature:* moderate (350–375°F., 180–190°C., Gas Mark
4–5)   ☐ *Serves:* 6–8
☐ *Freezing tips:* freeze on the serving plate and put into a polythene
container, or wrap carefully and place in a cake box. This makes
certain the cake is not crushed by other foods.   ☐ *Use within:* 2
months   ☐ *After freezing:* thaw out. At room temperature this takes
about 2 hours, but allow 5–6 hours in a refrigerator.

12 oz./300 g. chestnuts
Syrup
just under ½ pint/3 dl. water
2 oz./50 g. sugar
few drops vanilla essence or a
  vanilla pod
Sponge
2 eggs
3 oz./75 g. castor sugar

2 oz./50 g. self-raising flour, or
  plain flour and ½ teaspoon
  baking powder
Topping
1—2 tablespoons rum
¼—½ pint/1½—3 dl. thick cream
½—1 oz./15—25 g. castor sugar
1 oz./25 g. icing sugar

To cook
1 Slit the skins of the chestnuts and boil in water for just under 10 minutes. Remove the outer and inner skins while warm.
2 Put the shelled chestnuts into the washed saucepan with the water, sugar and vanilla essence or pod.
3 Simmer steadily for about 20—25 minutes until tender. Leave the chestnuts in the pan until stage 9.
4 Meanwhile whisk the eggs and sugar until thick, then fold in the sieved flour or flour and baking powder.
5 Grease and flour the sandwich tin, or line the bottom with greased greaseproof paper.
6 Pour the mixture into the tin and bake for approximately 15 minutes in a moderate oven until just firm to the touch; do not over-cook. Turn out and allow to cool.
7 Put the sponge on to the serving dish, then blend the rum with 2 tablespoons chestnut syrup. Spoon over the cake.
8 Whip the cream, add the sugar and spread carefully over cake.
9 Put the well drained chestnuts into sieve and press into a basin; add enough syrup from stage 3 to give a piping consistency and pipe into a spiral over the cream. Dust with sieved icing sugar.

Variation: Use canned chestnuts.

To freeze
Prepare the cake, freeze without wrapping. As soon as the gâteau is firmly frozen, wrap it.

Freezing sponge cakes: Delicate sponges, as the recipe above, freeze extremely well.

Egg custard

□ *Cooking time:* $1\frac{1}{2}$–2 hours for 1 large container, 40–45 minutes for small containers as shown in picture below.   □ *Preparation time:* few minutes   □ *Main cooking utensils:* ovenproof dish or dishes plus bain-marie and saucepan   □ *Oven temperature:* slow to very moderate (300–350°F., 150–180°C., Gas Mark 2–3)   □ *Serves:* 4
□ *Freezing tips:* see page 77

Some questions and answers

Q. Can you freeze eggs?
A. Raw eggs do not freeze in their shells; they 'break through' these; hard-boiled eggs are singularly unsuccessful when frozen — they are hard and leathery.
You can, however, freeze the yolks and whites of eggs separately so if you have a surplus of eggs, or if you have an opportunity to buy eggs cheaply, this is what I would do:
1 Separate the eggs. Beat several yolks with a little seasoning or sugar, put into a small container. Label the container with the number of egg yolks etc., e.g.

3 egg yolks + 2 teaspoons sugar

Put the whites into a separate container and mark the number. There is no need to season or sweeten these.
Egg yolks, or yolks plus whites, can be used in custards or sauces etc*. Egg whites can be used for meringues or mousse. Use within 8–9 months and thaw out thoroughly and slowly before using. To hasten defrosting stand containers in *cold* water.
2 If you would rather use the eggs in a dish there are many recipes in this book.

Individual custards can be cooked for the times given opposite. The proportions to use are 2–4 egg yolks or whole eggs (depending upon whether you like a lightly set or firm custard), 1 oz. (25 g.) sugar or seasoning to taste, 1 pint (6 dl.) milk, grated nutmeg for topping. Either steam, i.e. cook over hot, but not boiling, water, or bake, see times opposite and page 77; or *allow frozen custard to thaw out, pour into the top of a double saucepan and cook over hot water.

Q. Are there any kinds of food you cannot freeze successfully?
A. Salad ingredients, such as lettuce, watercress, radishes. Tomatoes cannot be frozen and remain firm, but they can be used in cooking (see page 31).
Mayonnaise tends to curdle, I generally advise people *not* to freeze this. If you have made a large quantity of mayonnaise and there is a risk of it being wasted I *would* freeze it and thaw out when required. If it has separated whisk it vigorously, or use it in a dip or salad where it would not be obvious.

Valentine cake

Cream 4 oz. (100 g.) margarine with 4 oz. (100 g.) castor sugar. Beat in 2 large eggs, then fold in 4 oz. (100 g.) self-raising flour (or plain flour with 1 teaspoon baking powder). Put into a large, well greased and floured heart-shaped tin and bake above the centre of a moderate oven, 350–375°F., 180–190°C. Gas Mark 4–5, until firm. This takes approximately 20 minutes. Cool the cake. Make an icing with 4 oz. (100 g.) margarine or butter, 8 oz. (200 g.) sieved icing sugar and 2 tablespoons orange juice. Coat the sides of the cake with part of this icing and 2 oz. (50 g.) chopped nuts. Spread a glacé icing (made with 6 oz. (150 g.) sieved icing sugar and 1 tablespoon orange juice) over the top of the cake and pipe a design with the remaining soft icing.

See the remarks opposite about freezing.

More questions and answers

Q. What kind of cakes can you freeze?
A. Light sponges, decorated gâteaux, in fact practically every kind of cake. I would not put very rich fruit cakes in the freezer as they keep so well in a tin, so it seems rather pointless. The decorated Victoria sponge opposite illustrates the advantage of freezing the type of cake that becomes stale quickly. You can make and decorate this *when* convenient and freeze it. Wrap it or put it into a container so the other foods will not press on the decorations (see page 119).

Q. If you freeze a decorated cake it would spoil the decorations if it was wrapped, but one is always told to wrap *before* freezing, what can you do?
A. There are a number of cakes, decorated desserts, etc., where you must freeze without covering, then cover when hard. I generally write myself a little note to remind myself to go and cover them within about 12 hours. The cake pictured opposite is a perfect example of food you must freeze first and wrap afterwards.

Q Why is there so much insistence on wrapping foods? What are the best things to buy?
A. Because the temperature inside the freezer not only freezes the food, but if food was left unwrapped it would dry this appreciably and so spoil the flavour. Unwrapped food could also have what is known as freezer burn, which could discolour the food and also adversely affect the flavour. Do not, however, become frightened by the thought of wrappings, etc., for if you look around your larder or refrigerator you may have a lot of Tupperware containers which are excellent in the freezer for you simply snap on the lids; these containers are available in many shapes and sizes. You may have flameproof ware, like Pyrosil – which is also good. You would need to cover the top only of the containers with double foil or freezer foil and seal this. When you buy special containers for your freezer remember these can be used again. I make use of an enormous amount of foil, and foil dishes which I use a number of times. Freezer-quality foil is heavier than we normally buy, but if you run out of this then use a double thickness of ordinary foil. The polythene you buy for the freezer should be heavier than is used for ordinary wrapping. There are many ways in which you can close polythene bags, etc., – by special freezer tape, which is not affected by the dampness, by special tags or,

if you want to become extremely professional, you can buy an appliance – a heat sealer – for sealing freezer bags.

Q. On page 23 you state you cannot freeze raw potatoes, what about chips?
A. The chipped potatoes are partially cooked *before* freezing (see page 35).

Q. What kind of foods would you select for freezing?
A. This is a difficult question as everyone has their own particular way of living, but these are the things I find more helpful to have in my freezer:
1 A selection of starters, see pages 8–18. This enables me to turn a family meal into a special occasion meal.
2 A selection of cooked main dishes, preferably those that can be heated through quickly. These are invaluable if ever I am delayed and have little time for cooking, see pages 20–74. Also a good selection of frozen vegetables too, (see pages 35, 71).
3 Some desserts of various kinds; pages 76–96 and 102–6 give ideas.
4 Tea time foods. As a family we eat tea rarely, but it is so helpful to have scones, etc., in the freezer, so you can issue invitations to people without any last minute fuss (see pages 108–121).
5 Bread and rolls – especially before holiday periods. One always seems to run out of bread at the most inconvenient moment (see pages 108–114).
6 Foods that are seasonal, i.e. soft fruits (see page 93) game (see page 53) fresh herbs (see page 21).
These are my first choice when filling my freezer, but in addition I like to have stock for sauces, gravy, etc. I like some uncooked meat and fish. I *never* waste any food, but use my home freezer as an extension of my refrigerator, i.e. foods that might spoil or deteriorate with normal storage time in the refrigerator (or the larder) go into the freezer – cheese (see page 29), sandwiches and left-over cooked meat are examples.
I also freeze for special occasions when I am likely to be very busy, i.e. parties, Christmas time, etc.

Q. Do you make ice in your freezer?
A. If you wish, or you can make ice in the freezing compartment of the refrigerator. Remove cubes from the trays, then pack the cubes in containers in the freezer – excellent if a large amount of ice is needed for the party.

Q. Why the emphasis on tight wrapping of poultry, etc?
A Because the tighter the wrapping the less air space, and the quicker the freezing and so the best results are obtained.

FREEZING SUBJECTS

In addition to the recipes indexed at the beginning of the book you will find information given on the following subjects.